Drive To Thrive
WHAT IT TAKES TO BECOME AN INSPIRATIONAL
MANAGER BY BRINGING THE BEST OUT OF OTHERS

SHARAD BAJAJ

DRIVE TO THRIVE
By: Sharad Bajaj

Published by:
Sharad Bajaj
Seattle, WA, USA

Copyright © 2020 Sharad Bajaj
All Rights Reserved
ISBN: 9798583979837

This book has been published with all efforts taken to make the material error free after the consent of the author. However, the author and publisher do not assume and hereby disclaim any liability to any party for any loss, damage or disruption caused by errors or omissions, weather such errors or omissions result from negligence, accident, or any other cause.

All rights reserved. No parts of this publication may be reproduced, distributed, or transmitted in any form or by any means electrical or mechanical including photocopy, recording or by any other information storage or retrieval system, without the written permission of the author. Expect in the case of brief quotations embodied in critical articles and reviews.

Help and Supported By Paper2Publish
www.paper2publish.co.in

DEDICATION

To my families who have always supported me and inspired me: Aarti Khanna, our parents and our children and special thanks to Ranjan Khurana and Anupam Khurana for the support.

To my second family, all of you those I worked with closely. In this book, you will find my 20 years of experience as story that will illustrate how each one of you helped me to shape my mindset, my career. I attempted to put all the learnings I had through all of you in past 20 years. The valuable experiences I had with all of you encouraged me to write this book. As you read this book, I want you to know that it's not just my experience, it's our experience. It's a story of one person finding a deep passion of leading people and applying it day-to-day in pursuit of bringing best out of others to deliver impact and building leaders. I hope that this book will inspire all of you to lead your team and business with compassion, courage, and vision. Thanks to all my current and past teammates for the ideas, discussions, encouragements and support. This book could not have been possible without you.

CONTENTS

Introduction: My Journey — I

Prologue – What's in this book?

Evolution Of Management – The History

1 Who Is A Manager? — 3

2 The Best Manager — 19

3 Hurdles Of A Manager — 45

4 Work-Life-Balance Is A Hoax — 77

5 Culture – Values and Habits — 89

6 White Space — 143

7 There Is No Map — 155

8 The Ultimate Choice — 167

9 Just Start – Bias for Action — 183

INTORDUCTION

It was a cloudy summer Wednesday in 2013; the sun was up early as always, sprinkling goldenness in its wake. I could hear birds from the distance chirping to the dawn of yet another day. As usual, I woke up early to prepare for the day's duties and to beat the morning traffic. I started my day with a cup of coffee and some positive affirmations and set off to work. On my way to the office, I got an email from my boss stating there were issues at the office that needed my immediate attention. Of course, I wasn't in any way perturbed, as it was part of the everyday hustle and bustle for me.

While I drove and thought of the issues, I got a call from my wife. She reminded me of the Parent-Teacher Meeting that was going to be held, and I needed to represent both of us at the meeting.

That rattled me, as both the meeting held at my kids' school and the office's urgent problem coincided. I was in a fix. While I contemplated how best to handle the situation, my tenant, who occupied one of my flats, texted to make a formal complaint about the faulty water tank, requiring urgent attention.

Now, I was in a dilemma. I had three pressing situations that required not just my time and attention but my physical presence. Then, I got a call from my mother, who clearly stated her displeasure over our recent lack of communication. I apologized profusely, but she insisted I called as soon as possible as we had important business to discuss. It was barely 9 a.m, but I was already fully booked. Was I frustrated?

Of course. I am human. However, I decided to approach these unplanned situations tactfully while still putting in my best to achieve excellence. In this book, I will share the techniques that I used to navigate these situations successfully. So, keep reading.

PROLOGUE

There are countless books on business, leadership, and management styles, from forgettable to timeless books. I will tell you what this book is not; this book is not just any other management or leadership style manual that regurgitates old information and compiles it in many pages. *Drive to Thrive* offers practical techniques that will help navigate, elevate, and enable you to take control of your personal and professional life. It also provides practical ways to manage your team effectively and keep them productive and motivated, especially in this era of remote work.

There is no doubt that the Coronavirus pandemic has taken its toll on us and has changed the way businesses and corporations operate as they all try to adapt and stay in the game. **Drive to Thrive** is a timely guide that seeks to help managers at all levels remain as integral and as competent as ever, even while managing their teams remotely.

Suppose you've purchased *Drive to Thrive*. In that case, you're an aspiring manager, or you've been frustrated in the past just like me, and you are searching for new ways to become a better manager, both personally and professionally.

You may be an intern, a seasoned professional, an executive, an entrepreneur, or someone who desires growth in their personal and professional lives while working remotely. In that case, you are holding the right book.

Drive to Thrive is a necessary reminder of what is required to attain managerial excellence. It takes you on a journey of discovering yourself as a manager and a leader by honing new skills and qualities that enable you to manage effectively. You can nurture a culture of excellence in your team and organization, lead a richer and more fulfilling life, and be more daring to take more risks.

I sincerely hope that each page in this book gives you a different perspective on managing your work, team, and life. I will share ideas, tips, and experiences that are not emphasized in schools or colleges.

EVOLUTION OF MANAGEMENT

Management itself is as old to man as the pyramids to Egypt. It has an ancient history leading up to the present times. The manager has been a history maker and has had relevance for a very long time. The manager's role would always be relevant because all organizations, be it small or large, at one point or another, have required assistance in implementing new undertakings and the supervision of projects. However diverse, these projects require a manager to ensure their proper completion and provide accountability and responsibility. As a leader, the manager sees the best in others and seeks to harness their potential.

I tell who cares to listen, "The manager is not the most powerful person in the organization. The manager is the most empowered person in the organization and can bring out the best in others."

In the "Project and People Management's" history, some significant developments and events adequately illustrate how much and how far the manager has come. A manager's duties have always been deemed essential, and one may refer to it as a "game-changer" in project management. Project management has been in existence since early civilization. In 2570BC, the Great Pyramid of Giza came to completion. The pharaohs built these pyramids through taskmasters and slaves, and to date, archaeologists argue how they were able to achieve this feat.

It should come as no surprise as ancient records show that managers had the tasks of overseeing the completion for each of the four faces of the great pyramid. It is now apparent that the Pharaohs combined planning, control, and execution in managing this project to see its fruition.

Another historic project that we can trace to having some form of management presence is the Great Wall of China, built in 208BC. According to historical data, the great wall's construction was a massive project requiring a large labor force. The labor force consisted of three parts; the soldiers, the commoners, and the criminals. From the look of things and the situation surrounding the events, the soldiers were the managers. They supervised daily work, allocated duties, and made sure the common goal was achieved.

In recent times, the need for a more pronounced structure led to project management's birth in the 19th century. While the taskmaster role may now be obsolete, there is a new leadership style, including budgeting and scheduling. With practice over the years, we have seen a whole new level of refinement and a shift in managing projects and people to achieve set goals.

It is safe to say that the word "manager" may not have been coined back in the day, much like many terms used now, just like the color orange didn't "exist" until the inception of its name. However, we can't take away the fact that orange flowers, orange fruit, did exist. All the structures and buildings back in the olden days required managers; otherwise, we wouldn't be seeing any ancient structures today. They all needed the presence of one person or a group of people who were ready to take charge and oversee the various projects.

There have been so many historical events leading up to why it can be historically proven that a manager's job isn't "new on the block," as we like to put it. Managers have and would always be required personally and professionally. Presidents, senators, law enforcement officials, and many more individuals in leadership positions are said to be managers.

They all manage situations in their different capacities. Management is an essential tool in surviving, and that is why a manager's job is crucial and necessary for growth and development in a given organization.

CHAPTER 1

WHO IS A MANAGER?

"A manager is a guide. They take a group of people and say, 'with you, I can make us a success; I can show you the way."

– Arsene Wenger

Whenever I get asked who a manager is and their duties and functions to the corporate world? I can't help but remember the story of my childhood and its role in my life.

Many years ago, my family and I lived in a small town in India. The community was warm, friendly, and everyone knew one another. The community school was a few miles away from our house, and I can vividly remember walking with the other kids to and from school every day. My siblings and I loved playing cricket afterward. I also remember my mother admonishing my siblings and me always to take care whenever we went out, which was her mantra each time we told her we were leaving home for some childish business. She would smile and say, "you all be careful and come back at sunset." Then, she'd tell me to watch over my siblings and make sure that they are safe.

In retrospect, those were the first of many times that I was entrusted with being responsible for myself and other people. My mother always ensured that I understood that I could guide and correct my younger siblings' actions as an older child. As I got older and took up more duties personally and professionally, I can see how my childhood shaped my leadership and management style.

Many questions plague the corporate world. One constant problem is who and what a manager is; is managerial duty earned through a professional degree alone, or is there more to being a manager? These are questions that beg for answers and have divided opinions in corporate and personal spaces.

So, who is a manager? A manager is many things; you may refer to them as a boss, a leader, a mentor, a team lead, and so much more. They can also be the person who gives you set deadlines on a project, offers guidance when you need it in the office, someone who talks too much at meetings to waste everyone's time, someone who designates meeting times, and so much more. The manager's role is vast and complex, and so, a manager can be many things to different people even within the same organization. In simple terms, a manager is a leader, much like the musical conductor of an orchestra.

A manager leads a department in an organization, manages the department's resources, has a task and responsibility to steer the department in the direction defined by its mission, vision, goals, and objectives. A manager has short-term and long-term targets to achieve and is responsible for them. Therefore, they must be equipped with the right knowledge and tools to be effective and productive.

At any point in life, you have the responsibility of managing. It could be managing oneself, family, finance, team, business enterprise, or organization. One thing is sure in management; if all the various components align with the organization's vision and mission, there is a high chance for success.

WHO IS MANAGER?

It is essential to understand what it means to be a manager and the roles and responsibilities required to be effective and get the best possible results at any given time.

Management requires both tact and nous. So, as a manager, there are specific tools that you must possess and employ to handle all parts of the management process effectively. If you manage a department, you will need every member of your team to fully understand what is required to achieve set goals and contribute positively to its growth.

But how can this be achieved? We will be discussing that in the latter part of this book.

"Managers are not the most powerful individuals in the company; they are the most empowered ones."

- Sharad Bajaj

Often, we tend to think of managers based on their positions in an organization. It is not unusual to feel this way, as it informs us about their roles and responsibilities in an organization. However, a manager's role broadly precedes organizational hierarchy and has morphed into a new part that is meaningful and enriching for everyone involved in an organization.

A manager then becomes a leader, a coach, a mentor, a friend, a coordinator, and so much more for the team they manage. Top managers serve, support, and empower their employees and other managers within an organization. By empowering others, they create an enabling environment where everyone can behave, think, and work independently.

I have had different opportunities to meet people and also conduct interviews. One of the many replies I get is, "I want to be a manager like you." It is an ambitious statement, no doubt, but it leaves me a little amused and with many mind-boggling questions. I always proceed to question their choices, and I almost always get the same kinds of replies. These replies revolve around wanting to be a manager is the financial gains they hope to attract or the consuming need for control. Yes, many people desire to be managers.

However, it is safe to assume that these misconceptions about the roles and duties could drive people to conclusions that may be detrimental to them and their organization in the long run. The need for control should not be an aspiration or goal for a person hoping to be a manager. Nelson Mandela properly illustrates this by saying,

"It is better to lead from behind and put others in front, especially when you celebrate victory when nice things occur. You take the front line when there is danger. Then people will appreciate your leadership."

"Managers, must inspire people to dream more, do more, be more."

- Sharad Bajaj

From the general perspective, as stated earlier, it is clear that the manager holds many responsibilities as they oversee the day-to-day activities and successful execution of a project within an organization. There is, however, more to a manager than a person who oversees activities. According to Rory Burke, "Project management can be defined as a way of developing structure in a complex project where independent variables of time, cost, resources, and human behavior come together." It is clear that as a manager, you are tasked and entrusted with the responsibility of bringing different resources together and making them work effectively and efficiently.

The above definition implies power and responsibility for a manager, and if not adequately checked, it might result in abuse. Nobody wants to work with a person that craves power and is controlling, and individual growth can never occur in a disgruntled team and a suffocating environment. A manager must be a team player, be accessible by everyone under you, and must inspire people to dream more, do more, be more.

Working as a manager is an accomplishment because it reveals a professional's ability to successfully lead, oversee multiple business operations, manage stress, and effectively communicate with co-workers. It is like cooking a pot of soup; you have different ingredients that come together to make it tasty. Chicken soup doesn't just only require chicken. It requires elements such as water, pepper, salt, seasoning cubes, and much more. These ingredients, when brought together, produce a delicious product. A manager must effectively bring diverse resources together to achieve an organizational goal.

I remember one incident at a company where the team members agreed to settle a small issue that could escalate if not adequately resolved. However, the manager stood against them because, to her, "she was the boss." Instead, she chose to go with her ideals. It turned out to be an epic failure, which was very embarrassing. The staff had an easy way out, but the manager couldn't bring herself to admitting or reasoning with her team.

As a manager heading a group of people, you must be willing to take diverse opinions and suggestions from others.

You must be ready to follow and listen to your team intentionally before making decisions because whatever stand or decision you make ends up affecting everyone in the group. It is also important to note that the manager's findings aren't a sole decision but a team decision.

Countless studies have been carried out to determine the core duties of a manager. However, few are as famous as the research of Professor Henry Mintzberg, which was carried out in the early 1970s. After studying individual managers for several weeks, Professor Henry asserted that managers assume various roles to meet the many demands of performing their functions. He identified ten roles that characterize the work of all managers. These roles can further be divided into three groups, namely:
- Interpersonal
- Informational
- Decisional

The interpersonal function ensures that adequate information is provided to inform a team's decisions and activities. It also covers interpersonal relationships between the manager and other group members and sets them in a unique position to get information.

In the interpersonal role, the manager acts as

Figurehead: they represent the organization formally. The top-level manager represents the company on social and legal matters outside the organization, while the supervisor is the intermediary between higher management and the workgroup.

WHO IS MANAGER?

Liaison personnel: they interact with people within and outside the organization. Top-level managers use this role to gain favors and information, while supervisors use the position to maintain workflow flow.

Leader role: In this role, managers ensure a good relationship between members of the organization.

The informational role ensures that the right information is disseminated across all organization levels, and it links all managerial work together. In the informational role, the manager acts as

Monitor: In this role, the manager receives and collects information.

Disseminator: In this role, the manager transmits unique and vital information into the organization. Top-level managers receive and share information from people outside of the organization to benefit the organization's growth. At the same time, the supervisor acts as the spokesperson within top management and the workgroup. Therefore, the top-level manager may be regarded as an industry expert, while the supervisor is a unit or departmental expert.

The decisional role takes the information, interprets it, and makes meaningful use of the data in the decisional role, the manager acts as

Entrepreneur: In this role, the manager initiates change and innovation within the organization.

Disturbance handler: In this role, the manager adequately deals with threats to the organization.

Resource allocator: In this role, the manager chooses where the organization's resources are expended.

Negotiator: As a negotiator, the manager negotiates business dealings on behalf of the organization.

The top-level managers make the organization's decisions as a whole, while the front-line manager makes the decisions about his or her particular work unit. The supervisor performs these managerial roles but with a different emphasis than higher managers. Supervisory management is more focused and short- term in outlook.

Thus, the figurehead role becomes less significant, and the disturbance handler role and negotiator roles become more important to the supervisor. Since leadership permeates all activities, the leader role is among the essential functions at all management levels. Therefore, whatever managerial capacity you occupy in an organization, it is necessary to understand that the organizational work is the lifeblood of an organization. You are tasked with the responsibility to inspire, motivate, lead, supervise, and delegate tasks in your team in order to achieve operational excellence.

The Organizational Process

As a manager, you must understand that you are an essential part and parcel of the organization, and you must ensure that you correctly translate and communicate information. Through daily planning, negotiation, implementing, defining performances and results, and creating a balance, you can ensure that resources are utilized efficiently in tandem with the set goals and objectives.

These duties may seem daunting to a new manager, no doubt. However, if there are adequate mechanisms set to checkmate the activities within the team or department you manage, it can be easy. Therefore, you must create an efficient process to utilize the tools at your disposal effectively.

Therefore, any manager's role is to piece different components and get the best resources available to ensure that they meet their goals and objectives. And, this means getting the right tools and personnel for any project. You must understand that different approaches and management styles are required to get the best from the available resources on a project at every point.

According to Marcus Lemonis, CEO of Camping World and serial entrepreneur, any business venture's success depends on three fundamental factors, also known as the three Ps of management: People, Process, and Product.

People

"If you pick the right people and allow them to spread their wings - and put compensation as a carrier behind it – you don't have to manage them."

- Jack Welch

A manager understands that people are the most crucial asset in any organization. Your employees are the live wire of your organization, and without them, nothing can be achieved within the organization. Therefore, you must equip them with adequate resources and a conducive working environment to ensure that you get the best results collectively and individually.

It is vital to get the right people in your team also, as it is almost impossible to achieve success in any organization without the right people performing the right tasks and at the right time. Good processes and products can only take you so far. So, the right kinds of people are needed for a business to truly thrive. However, it is noteworthy that what is right for one company may not be suitable for another, including personnel. Therefore, a manager is responsible for selecting the right team, ensures that they perform optimally, and marches them to success.

A manager must lead, inspire, influence, listen, connect, motivate, and show empathy towards team members. There must also be effective communication among all members to foster teamwork and a total understanding of assigned tasks.

Process

"If I had one hour to save the world, I would spend fifty-five minutes defining the problem and only five minutes finding the solution."

– Albert Einstein

The right process always helps a team to achieve their desired results. As a manager, you must understand that defining, developing, and delivering effective strategies adaptable to changing trends is just as important as delivering the final product. After the right people have been hired, well-thought-out methods must be in place to inform their work. Plans and strategies must be well-defined, understood, and communicated to all team members to follow. Delegation of tasks should be shared among team members to foster responsibility, accountability, and productivity. Implementation of strategies and milestone tracking is also essential to check the efficacy of any process adopted. We're often attached to getting results while being blindsided by the relevance of the process.

Therefore, a manager must provide the necessary direction and guidance to each individual and the team as a whole and a straightforward process that will act as a roadmap to steer and guide the team towards achieving set goals.

Product

"You've got to start with the customer experience and work back toward the technology – not the other way around."

- Steve Jobs

The ultimate aim of any organization is to create solutions for its customers by providing products and services that meet those needs. The outcome of the best people using the best processes is a great product. A product could be in a tangible form, such as an item or a tool. And at other times, it could be a service such as counseling, accounting, legal services, and much more. However, a great product is not the sole determinant of any business's success if it isn't relevant to the needs. A company may have a great product with zero sales because it doesn't solve real problems for people.

However, with efficient, well-engineered processes for delivering those products or services and a team of outstanding people to make sure it gets done and that customers are the priority, a great product can transform a business from struggling to thriving. Therefore, it is the manager's responsibility to ensure that all these factors are put in place to better the chances of success and sustain business growth and profitability in the long term.

WHO IS MANAGER?

CHAPTER SUMMARY

We discussed that a manager means many things to different people in an organization, and the managerial roles and responsibilities are vast and cut across all levels in an organization.

A manager is a leader, a boss, a leader, a mentor, a team lead, and so much more. They are in charge of a department in an organization, controls the department's resources, and has the responsibility to steer the department in the direction defined by its mission, vision, goals, and objectives. A manager has short-term and long-term targets to achieve and is answerable to them. Therefore, it must be equipped with the right knowledge and tools to be effective and productive.

It is also noteworthy that everyone manages at different capacities. However, a manager's role significantly precedes organizational hierarchy and has morphed into a position that is meaningful and enriching for everyone involved in an organization.

Management is not about control or financial gains; it is about being a part of a vision, leading a team towards that vision, and ensuring the successful execution of an organization's idea.

A manager's roles cut across all management levels, such as interpersonal, informational, and decisional.

As a manager, you must understand how to piece together diverse resources, like human and material resources, and ensure that they work in tandem to achieve organizational goals and objectives.

REFLECTION

How would your team describe your management style?
Reflect: _____

_____

_____
_____

_____

How do you prioritize tasks to ensure high productivity levels in your team?
Reflect: _____

_____

_____
_____

_____

Do you delegate tasks, or are you a do-it-all-alone type of manager?
Reflect: _____

_____

_____
_____

_____

CHAPTER 2

THE BEST MANAGER

"One of the quickest ways to gain someone's trust is to help them."

– Anonymous

My journey to becoming a manager always stemmed from a desire to help others achieve their goals and make a broader impact on my organization. I've always challenged myself to be a better leader, manager, and human being, and this conviction has helped me oversee and lead both small and large teams.

I can vividly recall many years ago after I became a senior engineer at Microsoft, I wanted to take on more responsibility. So, I approached my manager and asked for suggestions.

My manager stated that; "one way to make a broader impact in the organization is by first becoming a manager. This path involves collaboration, teamwork, understanding diversity, and much more. However, the best indicator of a manager's role is through the actions and leadership skills of the person," he opined.

I have led different teams, from four to a group of more than a hundred people. I have picked up so many lessons along the way, but one that stuck and has been beneficial is; the essence of trust.

Your team must trust you, and you must trust your team as well. You must nurture Teamfidence in the group.

Teamfidence is a term that is popular among my team. It means having mutual trust and belief in your team. When a group knows that there is mutual trust among all members, they put their heart and mind into their tasks, translating to better performances.

It is your responsibility to create an environment where team members can express their opinions freely, knowing they matter. I always ensure that these principles guide my team towards attaining specific goals.

Some time ago, we had an impromptu meeting on a Friday about handling a big project that required my team and me to modify an existing company's product and make a presentation to the CEO for approval within a tight deadline.

There was no doubt that this was a daunting task and one that would test my team's ability to deliver within a short period. As an individual contributor to the team, I saw this as an excellent opportunity to lead a significant project.

So, I reached out to my manager and requested to drive the project the following Monday. My manager hesitated because the project involved many people but gave me the nod to oversee the project.

When the project started, a few things became immediately apparent; I worked with people from different departments and skill sets. I had to interact and collaborate with diverse opinions and ideas, which was unsettling because there were some problematic team members.

However, I had to look past all of that and focus on the goal. I also informed the team that we all had shared ownership of the project, it wasn't about any individual, and so, we must all put our egos aside and work together towards achieving the goal. It was a truly learning opportunity for me and I learned many lessons from that experience.

After the successful execution of the project, I understood five things:
1. Trust is a crucial building block for all relationships and is critical in a team. A lack of trust can break down a group because it threatens productivity, creates a toxic culture, and shuts down communication. It also demotivates team members, which ultimately impacts the project. Working individually on a project is the easiest thing to do, but working with others is challenging.
2. Working in a team is always better than working alone, because a team consists of people with diverse ideas.
3. I understood the need for collaboration, teamwork, trust, and diversity in a team.
4. When you walk alone, you go fast. When you walk with others, you go far.
5. Feeling a deep sense of love and belonging are fundamental human needs. People are cognitively wired to love, be loved, and to belong. When these needs are not met, we don't function optimally. We break. We fall apart.

"When you attain personal success, you are happy, but when you empower others to achieve success, you gain fulfillment."

– **Sharad Bajaj**

As a manager, it is crucial to understand the difference between theory vs. reality in your everyday life, as things rarely play out how they are written down and explained. As I mentioned earlier, you must learn to become a situational leader because different situations will test your abilities differently. Managers and leaders are not born; they are made. Technical brilliance often sees people promoted into management and leadership roles even though they are not (yet) capable of performing. Effective people management is critical to ensuring a happy and engaged workplace for all.

As a manager, I realized and embraced the need to spend more time away from my desk, collaborate with my team, and earn their trust. How do I achieve this?

I always ensure to answer questions to my team members to unblock them and be accessible to team members without any excuse. I also seek to motivate, unlock people's potential, and lead through others so that they can grow faster.

As a manager, I feel incredibly motivated when my team is successful. The success of a team determines the success of a manager. I have made it a culture to ensure that everyone in my group has input on any project that we embark on, no matter how little their opinion and contribution is. I always assure my team that I am still open to questions, observations, and suggestions, as I do not know it.

The culture of transparency and open communication has benefited my team and me in various ways and has helped us achieve our goals faster. Presently, people no longer need traditional managers - at least not in the way companies define the role, as in actively managing people's activities.

Most employees need mentors, coaches, teachers, guides, facilitators, and trouble-shooters to lead them throughout their careers. Most of us need someone to help us with the barriers and roadblocks with whatever's hindering us from being our best selves. Great managers see it as their role to lead people through their challenges and help them become successful.

So, what are the qualities of the best manager?

QUALITIES OF THE BEST MANAGER

"Leadership is not a title; it is action." - Anonymous

Unfortunately, there is no single all-encompassing answer to whom the ideal manager is, managers should not have limits to their learning capacity. I like to believe that there is no end to becoming a good manager. You should continually get better.

A good manager's qualities vary and depend on numerous factors like; the type of company concerned, the strategy, goal, context, stakes, team, management, and many more.

However, there are common qualities good managers must share irrespective of the organization in which they work. Good managers are leaders that ensure that they get the best out of their teams.

Put, just as there is bound to be the right employee for the right job, there is a right manager for the right company, context, and team. Hence, being the "best" manager is a fully context-dependent notion. However, as earlier stated, these factors are numerous and should be considered necessary elements in becoming the best manager.

THE BEST MANAGER HAS A VISION AND LEARNS TO COMMUNICATE WITH CLARITY

"First comes thought; then organization of that thought into ideas and plans; then transforming those plans into reality. The beginning, as you will observe, is your imagination." Those were the words of famous author **Napoleon Hill**. To become the best manager is knowing how to convey the mission to others and proposing a straightforward way of thinking that can orient everybody's work. Managers must develop a clear vision and communicate with clarity so that it looks like the past and not the future. Having an idea is one thing, but it is another altogether to communicate with clarity.

"Vision is the ability to talk about the future with such clarity; it's as if we're talking about the past."

- Simon Sinek

My early morning routine starts with giving gratitude to God for a beautiful family, and an opportunity to lead and manage my team, along with a brief walk outside that gets me closer to nature. Followed by a delectable cup of coffee, my soul becomes filled with enthusiasm. When I am set to work, with my head bent over the paperwork for the day, I ensure to envision the work, understand it, and get what it requires of me. It is a mental exercise I have every morning before diving into my main job.

I have benefited immensely from a habit of gratitude; personally, and professionally. I also make sure to have a little staff briefing to keep my team on the right track. After all, it is useless if your team can't clearly understand your work and communication. And I must emphasize the word, "clearly."

Therefore, it is crucial that your team understands and shares the same vision, as it paints a picture of the future. A clear and shared vision also raises your team's hopes, expectations and inspires them. An inspired team can go over and beyond to execute a successful project. Clarity is underrated; however, it is an essential puzzle every manager must solve.

With no North Star, employees sail into the rocks. As a manager, you have to enroll employees in building that vision/strategy, don't impose it on them: the former commitment, the latter compliance. And be prepared to communicate it more often than you ever thought you could.

THE BEST MANAGER ADOPTS THE "NO SILO RULE"

A good manager always sees the big picture and ensures that employees work. As companies grow, there's always a potential for divisiveness, whether consciously or subconsciously as different departments and divisions are created within an organization, the tendency to compete against one another increases. They may lead to these departments working against one another's best interest in a bid to impress the manager. It then becomes an emotion-driven contest that harms the company. It is vital to check for this tendency by adopting the no silo rule.

You can do this by encouraging employees and managers also to see the picture and work collectively as one cohesive unit towards the good of the company. Elon Musk and Steve Jobs actively adopted the no silo rule to ensure that their companies work together as a unit rather than see themselves as individual divisions. It has had a significant impact on Tesla's and Apple's successes.

For example, when assembling a team to work on a new project, assign members of different departments to work together. If it's developing a new product, include at least one member from your finance, design, operations, and marketing departments-and vice versa to be part of the team. In this way, you foster a culture of cohesiveness instead of divisiveness.

It is also essential to cross-train employees in different departments. This is a great exercise to ensure that your team understands the interconnection between all departments in the organization; that one team's effort affects other groups. It helps individuals think critically and understand how the organization works together.

Lastly, if you and your team encounter some challenges on a project, share them. Ask for help, especially from people that work outside your department, to help you see beyond your limited perspective and promote innovative thinking. Sometimes, we need a fresh pair of eyes to see and solve problems differently.

For the no silo rule to work effectively, every member of the organization must be involved in the process. So, ensure that you and other managers are setting the right culture. Compensate those with high performance and those who assist others in performing highly.

Always reiterate that the only real bottom line that matters is the organization's bottom line. Adopting the no silo rule will improve individuals' collaboration in your organization and make emotions work for you instead of against you.

THE BEST MANAGER BUILDS THE BRIDGE

A good manager understands that they are a bridge between employees and the organization's strategic needs. They piece together the best resources and get the best hands to perform tasks in a company. It first starts with Talent Recruitment; this consists of hiring professionals through well-thought selection processes, in addition to the candidate's adequacy, previous experience, and training. The best managers evaluate the competencies of candidates to fill a position.

Another responsibility of a good manager is Talent Retention; this consists of offering professional incentives that are not entirely economical. A good manager must ensure that the best hands are adequately motivated, feel psychologically safe in the work environment, and achieve their goals with the company.

As a manager, you have to make the team, organization a pleasant place to work; doing this will ensure that you retain the right people, in the right positions, and with the right mindset. As a result, long-term success is guaranteed.

THE BEST MANAGER SHOULD BE AUTONOMOUS AND RESPONSIBLE

A great manager must be able to tackle decisions with his team without external influence. Most importantly, they must be capable of bearing the responsibility of those choices, be they good or bad. It is also crucial that you prioritize and develop your employees' autonomy while also empowering them.

Being autonomous means being unafraid of responsibility, taking a firm stance on issues even when alone with a given opinion, and accepting the consequences of such a decision. Being a leader often means having to face difficulties on your own, which is not a strength given to everyone.

I am faced with daily challenges every day at work that requires my utmost dedication. When it is time to take responsibility for actions, guess who shows up and covers up for the team? You thought, right.

As a good manager, you must be productive and results-oriented. Take your employees' productivity seriously and give them the tools to be productive, keeping the number of processes to a minimum. A good manager is a goal-getter, but they are also people-oriented.

They ensure that their team is productive at all times and that no one is left behind. It is also necessary that everyone sees the big picture and buys into the vision of the project. It is, therefore, essential for a manager to continually motivate their team.

Good managers also teach their team to be autonomous so that there is no need for micromanagement.

People loathe micromanagement. Research from empowerment expert Gretchen Spreitzer (University of Michigan) shows that empowered employees have higher job satisfaction and organizational commitment, which reduces turnover and increases performance and motivation. Also, supervisors who empower are seen as more influential and inspiring by their subordinates. Everyone wins when you learn to let go.

THE BEST MANAGER KNOWS WHEN AND HOW TO BE IN COMMAND

Being in command is never an easy feat, and you are likely to feel burdened sometimes. However, the manager keeps an eye on the goal, gives directives, makes judgment calls, tackles obstacles head-on, and manages their emotions. They are a role model to others and take a firm stance on some issues – often going against the status quo – and win others' trust. Not an easy feat indeed, but it is achievable. I always remind my team members that
"we succeed together or we learn together. Failure is not a part of it."

-Sharad Bajaj

Nothing is more harmful to a team than a captain without direction, who cannot settle conflicts, who refuses to see reality as it is, who can't bear criticism, and who won't answer for his or her actions. It is the perfect recipe for disaster and should not, in any way, be encouraged.

Learn to tell yourself positive affirmations. You can do the work, and you will succeed.

THE BEST MANAGER TAKES THE RIGHT DECISIONS AT THE RIGHT TIME

Citing the experience that I shared on the introductory page about that cloudy Wednesday morning, this is how I navigated through the demanding situations; one method that has virtually helped me over the years is prioritizing. That is understanding and attending to tasks according to their levels of importance. Another useful technique is, removing myself from the problem; that way, I can think and apply objective solutions to the problem, and this is what I did.

In this situation, I decided to be calm and apply emotional intelligence, handling each task according to priority. As a manager, I have realized that it is vital that you continuously evolve into a good leader. You should practice situational leadership every time because challenges arise unexpectedly in a manager's life. Therefore, you must prepare.

And so, I first resolved the urgent problem at the office that took a few hours. Upon completion and approval, my manager permitted me to head over to my kids' school. I attended the meeting while ensuring to contribute meaningfully and monitor my children's progress at school. Immediately that was over. I proceeded to my tenant's house to supervise the ongoing work to fix the water tank's leakage. I had phoned a professional plumber to inspect the damage while on the way to the children's school. During supervision, which took a few hours, I called my mom, and we had an hour-long conversation. That day alone taught me life lessons that have stayed with me and guided me throughout my entire career.

With every choice the best manager makes, they are conscious of the purpose it serves. For the best manager, the art of decision-making is an essential requirement of leadership. It is not to be toyed with due to the manager's choices and often is the very reason for their success or failure. I have been in tight spots where I felt stuck with two evils, and I had to take the lesser evil. However, it didn't make a choice less evil, and I had to deal with whatever consequence came up due to my preference.

It is crucial to make the best decision possible, but making it at the right moment is vital. Decision-making is one critical element that a manager faces every day. There are crucial questions you must ask yourself before making a decision. What do you intend to achieve? Why are you compelled to make the decision? Is there a desirable outcome that you are visualizing? If so, write it down immediately. Now, ask yourself, "if I make this decision, will it provide the outcome at the end (assuming everything goes as planned)?" If your answer is yes, you can go to the next step. If your answer is no, spend some time clarifying the possible outcome.

Good managers always keep the end in mind before deciding, defining the necessary steps to take before making a decision, and always provide alternatives for their team's findings and business. The alternative to a lack of decision-making is indecision, which paralyzes an organization, creates doubt, uncertainty, lack of focus, and even resentment. Healthy decisions come from a strong sense of self-confidence and belief that a decision is better than none, even if proved wrong.

THE BEST MANAGER SHOWS MANAGERIAL COURAGE

One of the main qualities of the best manager is his managerial courage. After all, they must face problems, say things as they are, make difficult decisions, and be responsible for their actions. Recognizing things for what they are means saying that which needs to be said at the right time, to the right person, and in the proper manner. Agha Hasan Abedi says,

"The conventional definition of management is getting work done through people, but real management is developing people through work."

Courage is not some deep internal superpower that you can dig deep and suddenly discover. Courage, more than not, is external. Our courage stems from the support we feel from others. In other words, when you know that someone has your back when you fall, or someone says, "I gotcha, you can do this," when you are faced with a daunting challenge, that is what gives you the courage to overcome difficulties.

Courage is not going off to an Ashram by yourself for four weeks and coming back, having found it. It comes from the relationships you foster and the people around you who love, care, and believe in you. When you have these relationships, you will find the courage to do the right things. And, when you face challenges with courage, that, in turn, will inspire those in your organization to do the same.

So, courage is mostly influenced by external factors. The same can be said of inspiration. Does your courage inspire your team?

Making the right decisions in the face of overwhelming pressure are traits leaders with courage possess. Good managers also endeavor to get results through their team consistently. They have high standards for inputs, outputs, and outcomes. They aren't satisfied with just meeting the minimum permissible bar for metrics, product quality, customer satisfaction, and team collaboration.

Managerial courage means knowing how to manage the storm, including the incertitude and ambiguity that comes along with it. In the jungle, the elephant is the biggest; the giraffe is the tallest, the fox is the cleverest, the cheetah is the fastest; however, the lion is the KING of the jungle without having the best of these qualities. Why is that?

The answer is because the lion is courageous, bold, walks with confidence, and isn't afraid. The lion believes that it is unstoppable; it takes a risk and believes that every animal is food. The lion targets its prey and doesn't let the opportunity slip away.

>So, the key takeaways are;
>You don't have to be the fastest.
>You don't have to be the wisest.
>You don't have to be the biggest.
>All you need is;
>Courage.
>The willingness to try.
>Faith and belief in yourself.
>The mindset of possibilities.

The best manager is to make the right decisions, despite little or no information. Your team looks up to you. Your outlook on issues faced or presented becomes the entire team's outlook on that particular issue or situation. You must remember to carry a positive mindset.

I always think of Paul Tournier's words that say, *"Sooner or later, those who win are those who think they can."* It has become a silent mantra I chant when faced with challenges. Good managers are optimistic & secure in their role. They have a mature attitude and avoid pettiness. They know it's fair to express vulnerability. They say "I don't know" when that's true. They love learning. They exude presence.

THE BEST MANAGER SHOWS LEADERSHIP AND INSPIRES OTHERS

"Leaders must inspire others to dream more, learn more, do more, and become more."

- Sharad Bajaj

Leadership is entertaining a relationship of mutual trust. It is the culture of growth, the culture of working together, and the culture of teamwork. A manager also means being in charge, taking command, having vision, goals, and encouraging employee relationships and motivation while obtaining the group's collaboration with the primary objective in mind. I always make sure to be an inspiration to my team members every day, and it goes way beyond the work table. Encouragements can also come from you. You should remember that as a leader, you are a servant. I make sure to drop in compliments and check-ins. "Hey Sam, your submission last week was superb. Keep going." – is an example of a simple yet great compliment that can encourage Sam to better next time.

Good managers also put their team members above their self-interest when the two conflict. Also, they understand that the long game is all about people. They put an individual's mental & physical well-being above short term OKRs & results. They pay keen attention to a team member's feelings in addition to their spoken words and can detect dissonance between the two.

As the best manager, you are a coach and an inspiration to your team. You either care about your employees, or you don't. There's no gray zone. If you care, then you'll invest time and energy to help your employees become better versions of themselves. That's the first 50 percent of being a good coach.

The other half is knowing you're a facilitator, not a fixer. Ask the right questions; don't just give the answers. Expand your coach's point of view versus giving it to them. Sure, I'm oversimplifying, but not much.

"Leadership is all about inspiring others. Just add others after each of these words; coaching, inspiring, developing, growing, and caring."

– Sharad Bajaj

The best managers care about their people's careers and development as much as they care about their own. People crave feedback. And you owe it to them.

Good managers are proactive about their team members' career growth. They don't dread career conversations with team members; they actively invite such conversations. People don't work to achieve a 20 percent return on assets or any other numerical goal. They work to bring meaning into their lives, and purpose comes from personal growth and development. Good managers perform these tasks because they were once in their team members' position and managers acted as guides to inform decisions.

Google is an excellent example of a company that urges its managers to have vital technical skills (like coding), so they can share the "been there, done that" experience. So be there and do that to build up your core expertise, whatever that might be. Stay current on industry trends and research everything you can.

THE BEST MANAGER THINKS CLEARLY AND BRINGS CLARITY

A manager must help their team understand their responsibilities better. It may seem like basic knowledge, but it is vital that every team member fully comprehends their roles and sees how it contributes to the big picture. The best managers don't assign responsibilities to their team and leave it; they often talk with the group members about their tasks' progress and suggest efficient ways to ensure success. Good managers are skilled at asking questions that give their team members a new perspective on the problem and independently reach the right solution.

Also, as the best manager, you must be an excellent communicator. The biggest problem with communication is the illusion that it has taken place. It often doesn't happen because of a lack of effort from both the transmitting and the receiving parties. Invest in communication, and care enough to listen. Former CEO of Procter & Gamble A.G. Lafley once told his job was 90 percent communication--communicating the next point especially.

Good managers value clear thinking, sound judgment, and wisdom. They try their best but also realize they (and others) are fallible, and anyone can have a bad day. They know that their growth as a manager isn't a binary value; it's a continuous process.

THE BEST MANAGER FOSTERS AN INCLUSIVE AND PSYCHOLOGICALLY SAFE CULTURE

Good managers foster an inclusive culture in their teams to ensure that they have diverse perspectives to build products for various people. For example, a company that sells its products to people of different races and cultural backgrounds must have a diverse workforce as possible to best understand how best to serve their customers. Every voice matters in a team where diversity and inclusion thrive, and this is immensely beneficial in making the right decisions in a group. There is no gender, age, sexuality, color, or background bias when there is a culture of inclusivity.

Good managers also build productive relationships with their peers and senior company leadership because they know that's essential in helping their team members achieve their goals. Individual fulfillment is often a joint effort. People derive tremendous joy from being part of a winning team. The best managers facilitate the esprit de corps and interdependence. Naturally, employees positively respond to managers concerned about winning and winning well (in a way that supports their well-being).

It is also vital that as a manager, you foster a psychologically safe working environment for your team to attain success. Psychological safety can make or break a team. When people feel unsafe, they are inclined to take little or no risks, and this fear prevents employees from speaking up, providing honest feedback, or sharing their ideas. When your team feels psychologically safe, they can express themselves and provide opinions without fear of consequences of career or self-image. In a psychologically safe group, all members feel accepted, valid, and respected.

THE BEST MANAGER COLLABORATES

In a global and remote business world, collaboration skills are essential. Collaboration happens when each team member feels accountability and interdependence with other teammates. Nothing is more destructive for a team than a leader who is unwilling to collaborate. It creates an "it's up to only us" vibe that kills culture, productivity, and results.

Also, good managers don't have just one go-to management style, nor do they have a notion of "THE ideal employee." Good managers aim to create an inclusive & optimal environment for each individual, based on their specific strengths, weaknesses, preferred style of learning & working. In this way, collaboration works best.

THE BEST MANAGER IS AN EMPATH

"Empathy is about finding echoes of another person in yourself."

-Mohsin Hamid

What an incredible quality empathy is. I could talk about its benefits for ages. It is such an impactful gift and a requirement for all human beings, whether or not they belong to the corporate world. When I used to work at Microsoft, I had a critical deadline at work sometimes, and my team and I were working round the clock into late nights. Everyone was putting in their best, and I observed that a particular co-worker was withdrawn and wasn't delivering as usual.

After work had closed for that specific day, I walked up to this person to find out the problem. After a simple conversation, I got to learn his mom was terminally ill at the hospital. I immediately offered my apologies and condolences as I offered to cut the person some slack while we as a team covered up for whatever lapses there would be. With tears in his eyes, he thanked me profusely, and we shook hands.

Laying on my bed that night, I realized that we all had lives outside work, and just like other human beings around us, we also faced personal problems. I resolved to do my best to make sure kindness and empathy were my watchwords from that day forward.

One of the essential sentiments a leader can express to people they work with is, "I've got your back. There is nothing you can break that I can't help fix back together. I believe in you even when you don't believe in yourself." Empathy - the ability to recognize and share other people's feelings - is the most vital instrument in a leader's toolbox. The daily practice of putting other people's well-being first has a compounding and reciprocal effect on relationships, friendships, and the way we treat our customers and colleagues.

As a manager, empathy is a trait you must possess. It would be best if you also remembered that your team members are also humans with valid feelings and needs. However, do not confuse empathy with sympathy. Sympathy simply refers to the ability to take part in someone else's feelings, mostly by feeling sorrowful about their misfortune. On the other hand, empathy is the ability to understand other people's emotions as if they are our own. The corporate world barely teaches compassion; however, emotional intelligence must be learned and understood. An empathic manager makes for the best team leader. As an employee, you are hired based on your I.Q but grow based on your E.Q. It is challenging to grow in a fast-paced environment; you need to manage your emotions appropriately and use them to grow professionally. As much as a high I.Q may have gotten you a placement within an organization, a high emotional quotient is crucial to climbing up the organization's ladder. Having a positive attitude and maintaining motivation leads to growth; skills alone will not guarantee that. Emotional intelligence in the workplace will take you beyond the point where talent cannot reach.

WHEN HUMILITY AND VULNERABILITY IS STRENGTH

"Be humble, recognize that you don't know everything, and be willing to learn from others."

– **Sharad Bajaj**

C. S. Lewis was not wrong to say, "humility is not thinking less of yourself; it is thinking of yourself less." Having the courage to be vulnerable as a manager, the courage to be yourself, is the keystone of an inspiring leader. Humility is vital. Vulnerability, on the other hand, is having the courage to show that you are not perfect. It is living your truth and allowing yourself to be teachable.

Being the best manager requires you to recognize your weaknesses, mistakes, and to allow yourself to be corrected and teachable. Humility means acknowledging your errors without excuses, learning to put others at ease, encouraging and respecting different points of view, encouraging and supporting change, and surrounding yourself with people who are often better than yourself.

CHAPTER SUMMARY

We discussed the different roles, duties, and attributes of a good manager, and we stated that leadership is not just a role but an action. The duties of a manager are vital to the success of the company.

As a good manager, you must take responsibility for the success and failure of your team.

- You must be a visionary and transmit that vision to your team.
- As a good manager, you must motivate, inspire, and lead through others.
- You guide your team to success by creating an effective communication and feedback mechanism.
    o As a good manager, you must give purpose to a group of people and transform them into a team of dedicated individuals.
    o You must be fully vested in your team's career growth and develop strategies, actionable plans, and opportunities.
    o The best managers strive for diversity and inclusivity in their teams to ensure that they consider diverse opinions. It dramatically benefits and informs their organization in making decisions for products.
    o To ensure that everyone feels comfortable to share their perspectives without fear, a good manager must create a psychologically-safe culture for their team to achieve success.
    o A good manager must possess a high level of emotional intelligence to understand all team

members' needs, challenges, strengths, and weaknesses.
- As a manager, the journey to becoming the best manager has no end; as a manager, you must continually improve.

REFLECTIONS

What are your greatest strengths as a manager?
Reflect: _____

_____

_____

_____

What are your greatest weaknesses as a manager?
Reflect: _____

_____

_____

_____

What are you doing to Are you vested in your team's growth?
Reflect: _____

_____

_____

_____

CHAPTER 3

HURDLES OF A MANAGER

"Failure is a fact of life."

A famous quote by American business magnate Steve Jobs lives continually with me. It is a quote I carry along as a mantra every day of my professional life. I don't only love the simplicity of this quote, but I also love its realistic approach that speaks to my life. It says, "**sometimes when you innovate, you make mistakes. It is best to admit them quickly and get on with improving your other innovations.**"

This powerful quote continually reminds me that mistakes and struggles are inevitable parts of one's life; failures are a part of success. The hurdles we face are stepping stones to becoming an improved version of ourselves. This improved version introduces us to gain deeper insights into problem-solving and solution-finding.

Every human being is bound to face one hurdle or the other at some point in their lives. Sometimes these hurdles are a constant feature that requires immediate attention to propel us forward. Limitations are like stones on a pathway. You would have to learn to not only move them out of the way safely, but you would also need to study the patterns in which they appear to avoid a repetition in the future. Samuel Beckett says that

"**Ever tried. Ever failed. No matter. Try again. Fail again. Fail better.**"

This is a simple saying by Samuel Beckett that properly exemplifies that hurdles are day to day struggles that everyone would go through. What exempts you from others, and makes you stand out, is that you need to try continually. It includes whether you keep failing. You have to keep moving and be a problem solver.

Managers are no exception to hurdles. In fact, as a manager, you are faced with constant challenges almost every day of your professional life. These challenges constitute resource and people management. These tasks all come with their problems. Some of these problems might be new and require you to come up with novel and innovative solutions. If you are that manager who assumes managerial duties are easy because you are the boss, you might be living a colossal lie.

A manager's responsibilities are tasking, and specific dilemmas and situations require the manager's immediate attention. Timely solutions must be provided and must solve the posing problem to a considerable measure. The manager is like a track athlete; they have the audience looking forward to their victory, track team members banking on them, sponsors who hope they are not let down, and finally, other competitors they must outrun. These are enough pressures, and then they have the hurdles of jumping over to get to the finishing line.

The audience is his customer. The track team members are the team or co-workers. The sponsor is the boss, and the other track runners are fellow managers.

The manager has to properly blend these four ingredients in the right proportion while making sure to cross the hurdles set in front correctly. These hurdles include; deadlines, teamwork, customer service, the satisfaction of the organization's set goals, and many more.

"Happiness does not come from doing easy work but from the afterglow of satisfaction that comes after the achievement of a difficult task that demanded our best"
- Theodore Isaac Rubin

I often recall my early days as a manager. New to the managerial world, young and inexperienced, I thought the world was at my feet. I had become the boss, which meant no hassle, pressure, or stress. I laugh now, thinking about my naivety back then. Well, I was jolted back to reality in no time, and I discovered that being a manager is no walk in the park and did not exempt me from the numerous hurdles and challenges I assumed I had grown past. The challenges only got more challenging and complex, and I needed to adopt innovative solutions.

These challenges propelled me to work harder as a manager to ensure that I applied the right answers in any situation. The challenges ultimately molded me to be the manager that I am today. When I complete a daunting task, the results are far more fulfilling, and the experience is far more enriching.

I would love for every person out there to truly challenge themselves to make the tough choices. Yes, you might fail, but in that failure lies a lesson learned. Therefore, you aren't failing but learning to do things better.

Whenever you encounter a new challenge in your life, always remember that progress is more important than the outcome. The process is infinitely more valuable and important than the result. When you commit to the process — never giving up, always overcoming setbacks and challenges, trying new ways — a powerful metamorphosis happens. You literally transform in the process. This change is the real value.

People who "just want the prize" miss this entirely. They don't realize how valuable and powerful the transformation is, which is only possible from taking the hard way around.

Now, let's look at the hurdles of a manager. However peculiar they might seem; these hurdles have solutions and an appropriate way of applying the situations.

POOR COMMUNICATION

To effectively communicate, we must realize that we are all different in how we perceive the world and use this understanding as a guide to our communication with others. Often, we ignore the power of proper communication. Communication is not just the passing of information; it is the passing of understandable information well received by the respondent. It goes beyond this by seeking feedback that shows communication was well received. And, just like feedback, communication is a two-way street.

Poor communication is one hurdle most managers face regularly and often do not know how to handle. There are cases where I have had meetings and communicated certain things to my team members, only for them to return to their desks, completely misunderstanding the message transmitted. As a result, they submit poor and shoddy jobs or half-done tasks without piecing together the tasks demand's necessary components.

Clear communication and clarity are vital in any organization. I can't stress this enough. After observing what a lack of proper communication does to team members and work outcome, I devised a means for team members to send back feedback in whatever medium they preferred, via emails, verbal communication, or alternative ways. As a manager, you must always encourage your team members to speak freely and respectfully. Oral communication does not work every time. Therefore, as a manager, you must create varied avenues that foster effective communication.

Also, encourage your team members to understand why they are carrying out specific tasks, how those tasks and the consequences of performing such functions on the business. Learn to properly communicate dates, repeat meetings if you have to, communicate the problem's scope, and ask for feedback to ensure your message has properly cut through. Communication is vital to personal and career success.

PERSONAL CHALLENGES INFLUENCE WORK

"Employees are a company's greatest assets-they are your competitive advantage. You want to attract and retain the best; provide them with encouragement, stimulus, and make them feel that they are an integral part of the company's mission."

- Anne M Mulcahy

I always remind my team members that they matter, and they are human beings as well. It is best to remember this as a manager. Everyone has personal problems, and sometimes these problems might begin to show a manifestation in one's work. It is your duty as a manager to identify these problems and seek immediate solutions. It is best to remember not to pry into their personal experiences unprofessionally, but suggesting things such as a day off, team retreats, and so much more can improve your team members' emotional and physical well-being.

We all are in the pursuit of making a business impact,

but at the same time, we are all trying to predict the future and plan for it. Some parts are unexpected, but we need to find solutions for them. Unpredictability is sure to arise, and when it does, it will do you right as a manager to be able to tackle it accordingly while taking lessons that would help for the future. It would be best if you also remembered to take care of your problems as a manager, so it doesn't affect the organization's day-to-day activities.

WORKING WITH FEWER RESOURCES

It is perhaps an essential hurdle a manager would have to face. It is crucial because this hurdle is one of the best challenges to test a manager's ability to be innovative and ingenious, but we struggle a lot with it. Every manager would always be faced with fewer resources to work with, and most times, many managers think the simple and straightforward answer is to ask for more help or more resources. We always need more, more, and more! Sure, it would be nice to have more, but more doesn't automatically translate to a better outcome. The managerial duties come with much stress attached.

When handling work problems, you start by defining the problem and seeking immediate answers to it. A mantra you should stick to is, "I need to learn how to do more with less." Doing more with less doesn't mean overworking your team members; it doesn't imply working. It simply means creating and building efficiency in the team. It means fostering a learning culture where people learn together and learn from others' mistakes. You are fostering a culture of cross-multiplication. And, as a manager, you should expect the challenge of doing more with less, even embrace it.

Organizations would always expect you to deliver more with less. It is a constant challenge, and I like that because it forces you to think outside the box and creatively develop new solutions.

There should be no need for team burn-out, and you should try to maintain the team's work balance. So, doing more with less requires adequate planning and handling to produce a desirable result.

THE TWO WORLDS BETWEEN THE TEAM MEMBERS AND THE CUSTOMERS

"A manager's first customer is their team; equip them well to function efficiently."

– Sharad Bajaj

There has to be a reconciliation between both worlds, as they both affect each other's performance directly. You need to make sure your team is doing great work and delivering on time. At the same time, the customers are receiving great value from their patronage.

Never ignore how you are putting your team on a project to achieve growth and success in their assigned duties and career goals. I always say, "people are a manager's best asset.".

Managers needs to continually challenge themselves to meet the needs of the first customer. The first customer is the team. In turn, they can better serve customers.

GROWING AS A MANAGER

"Comfort zones are beautiful places, but nothing ever grows there – get out of your comfort zone"

As a manager, personal growth is non-negotiable. Your development results would ultimately reflect in your life's decisions, and as such, you must strive for excellence to continually grow as a person.

You would face situations that challenge growth. These situations may be uncomfortable and would require you to leave your comfort zone. Leaving your comfort zone is not as scary an experience as it seems. It is a beautiful experience to engage. You would witness new changes. You would need to handle these changes as well as you can.

A step-by-step process takes you to your destination. As a manager, you will encounter many hurdles in your life. What will set you apart is your ability to handle these challenges while seeking to achieve a desirable result. Hold on to the words of Zig Ziglar, who said: "**What you get by achieving your goals is not as important as what you become by achieving your goals.**"

EFFECTIVE ONE-TO-ONE

One-on-one meetings with your team are the best way to learn about each member of the group. As a manager, you must understand that a one-on-one meeting is the employee's time. The frequency of these meetings also helps determine how much information you get from each team member. You must also ensure that the time allocated for these meetings meet the expectations of both parties.

I always advise my team to come with a plan for discussion in our one-on-one sessions, including career goals and self-improvement, interpersonal issues, and much more. Practical one-on-one happens when there is a clear objective or picture of what we will discuss. As a manager, it offers you a superb opportunity to know each member of your team better, and so, you shouldn't ignore its relevance in building a strong team culture. I also adopt the "two ears, one mouth" rule when I am having these meetings because it is crucial to listen more and talk less when your team members discuss their career growth and how you can help them achieve success.

The understanding of the manager-employee relationship is vital. If managers don't know about their team's interests, professional development, and career objectives, any efforts to help may be futile.

One way to foster a healthy relationship with your team as a manager is by having monthly career sessions to engage and know more about their goals. Such cadence shows a sustained interest in your team's development and allows you to have up-to-date perceptions from their direct reports. As a manager, it is impossible to know how you can help employees develop further without frequent career sessions and conversations.

Additionally, during one-on-one sessions, a manager must be a good listener. You have one mouth, two ears for a reason. It is vital to listen and observe more.

WE HAVE TWO EARS, AND ONE MOUTH SO THAT WE CAN LISTEN TWICE AS MUCH AS WE SPEAK.

When we speak, we share what we know; when we listen, we learn new information. What managers must understand is that there's always further information; they just have to listen more. Most managers generally like to talk about themselves and their struggles. When we do this, our ego gets in the way and clouds our judgment because we speak instead of listening.

FEEDBACK AND FOLLOW UP

"Feedback is like an unpolished diamond; to the untrained eye, a freshly mined gem may not look valuable, or even attractive."

– **Anonymous**

We would all like to believe that we respond well to feedback. We learn and change when we hear it because we are always striving to be better. But leaders are just like everybody else; feedback makes us defensive; our first impulse is self-protection and defection. We shield ourselves and then throw the feedback to the sender - maybe that's why it's called "feed it back."

Useful feedback is a big part of the growth mindset. Good managers know how to give feedback, it must be specific and actionable, and its context must be fresh. It is vital to provide feedback in real-time instead of waiting for monthly or yearly reviews. You should give feedback in a way that doesn't come off as an attack on a person; it must be constructive. Also, feedback is a two-way street; receiving and giving. As a manager, you must ensure that people feel safe to provide and welcome your feedback.

Every task in the plan must be subject to review, and adequate feedback by key individuals involved in performing tasks is essential. This way, it ensures that no member of the team is loafing around and accumulating excess workload. If this happens, it causes more extended completion of a project than initially planned.

Feedback must be honest and offered in real-time. One must be careful not to overstate the level of progress reached to know precisely where the team stands in achieving the objective and how to get there. It can also help identify challenges that may exist amongst your team members to troubleshoot immediately.

Compliment people regularly and in a meaningful way, not only to their faces but behind their backs so that people know you are sincere in your compliments and that you have faith in your direct reports. It builds trust, which, in turn, ensures people feel confident about sharing crazy ideas with you.

Managers who continually criticize their direct reports destroy trust. Why share a novel idea with a boss you know will attack it and possibly blame you as well? It is safer to keep your head down and follow the status quo to minimize criticism. When you need to criticize people, start with a compliment, ensure the criticism focuses on their actions rather than them, and be meaningful in your complaint. If possible, add a challenge to the end of the criticism.

Offer criticism constructively and in a way that an individual does not feel attacked. In identifying a problem with how individuals perform their given duties, it is crucial to have an effective one on one, rather than reprimanding the individual openly. In this way, you can safely guide the individual by applying corrective measures without killing their morale.

A person will go out of their way to work for a leader who makes them feel appreciated. Always point out the things that they do right. A simple "good job!" goes a long way in boosting confidence and inspires them to outdo themselves in the next assignment.

As a manager, providing ongoing constructive feedback is a great way to let your team members know how they perform and what you expect from them. It is very crucial, especially when they aren't performing at their best. For a manager, this may be a slippery slope in effectively handling their team remotely. There are specific points I always recommend to any manager that manages a team remotely:

I always recommend a face-to-face communication channel. As a manager, do not send a text to relay your feedback; it could easily be misinterpreted, and its effect may wane. I always ask an employee for a quick informal chat over a video call, which is the closest to face-to-face communication. In this way, I can see visual cues of how they react and discuss the problem extensively.

I also ensure that I get straight to the point. I do not beat around the bush, and I use straightforward language to explain the problem immediately. As a manager, this is important so that your employee is not under any illusion that the call is about something else. Ask them for their solutions and opinions, making sure to listen to what they say actively. When you have agreed on a decision, ask them to tell you what plan they have to ensure they've understood what is expected from them.

Body language signs are very crucial during feedback. Before the Coronavirus, a manager could read and interpret their team's body language whenever they are addressed. Presently, this is not entirely possible. Over video, it may be challenging to pick up an emotion.

As a manager, to ensure that you're sending the right message, you should appear calm and concerned - it will help you convey the issue's seriousness. There is an inevitable delay of speech on virtual meetings, which may cut off the end of sentences and give a notion of you not listening. Therefore, make a conscious effort of actively listening and taking short breaks between sentences to give your team a chance to speak - as it can be very easy to talk over one another.

Listening shows that you care about their concerns and presents an opportunity for them to express their ideas that may be part of the solution.

Timing is crucial in giving constructive feedback. Ensure you are calm before speaking to a team member about something negative to ensure that your feedback is objective and thoughtful. Focus on the problem, not the individual. Point out impartial observations and outcomes rather than the individual's attributes. This may be portrayed as a personal attack, resulting in them not being motivated to address the problem.

Lastly, you should learn to mix positive comments while pointing out the negatives. It tells your employee that you aren't criticizing their overall performance, just some particular parts.

CHANGES IN MANAGEMENT STYLE

The COVID-19 pandemic has forced new ways of working for companies all over the world. According to the McKinsey research, as of April, 62 percent of employed Americans worked at home during the crisis, compared with about 25 percent a couple of years ago.

A new study on pandemic-induced remote workers and their employers by Harvard Business School Assistant Professor Zoe Cullen and Associate Professors Michael Luca and Christopher Stanton suggest that 16 percent will remain at-home workers, long after the COVID-19 crisis has receded. The survey was on 1800 people in both small and larger businesses also found;

While overall levels of remote work are high, there is considerable variation across industries. Remote work is much more common in industries with better educated and better-paid workers.

Respondents in better educated and higher paid industries have also observed less productivity loss from the transition to remote work.

More than one-third of firms that had employees switch to remote work believe that it will remain more common at their company even after the COVID-19 crisis ends.

"These estimates suggest that at least 16 percent of American workers will switch from professional offices to working at home at least two days per week as a result of COVID- 19," the researchers conclude. "This would represent a dramatic and persistent shift in workplace norms around remote work, and has implications for companies, employees, and policymakers alike."

Virtual management and supervision are a few things managers have had to embrace in the COVID-19 era as it canceled out direct supervision of staff and teams. Thus, leaders have had to adopt many virtual communication tools and train themselves to use them effectively. Regular emails and memos are no longer enough to communicate and get feedback properly; the need for computer and mobile applications such as Zoom, Slack, WhatsApp, and Microsoft Teams have significantly increased in the absence of face-to-face interaction. Team briefings are via video conferencing, and feedback is through social media. While the pandemic gave room for management evolution, it also created some inevitable challenges for managers, which are:

- Lack of direct supervision of staff
- Delayed feedback
- Increased difficulty in communicating with teams
- Lack of a proper standard with which to measure team engagement
- Inability to offer a psychologically safe environment to staff
- Reduced control over the enforcement of standard operating procedure
- Failure to foster an appropriate interaction and interdependence between staff

To adjust to the changes in management styles brought on by the pandemic, consider these steps:

- Focus more on results rather than the procedure
- Encourage twice as much.
- Reaffirm your trust in your team and their abilities
- Provide employees with the necessary tools they need to work effectively in their remote environment.
- In providing remote work, tools identify problems within their environment that could pose a challenge to their work and help them overcome them by offering alternatives.
- Encourage the unconventional or out-of-the-

box approach to reach an objective.
- Invest time in promoting interaction and dialogue within your team
- Shed constant light on the organizational culture
- Set clear objectives and day to day goals
- Do not overwhelm them with outrageous expectations and set reasonable goals.
- Be patient and sensitive to their situations as they may be under more stress than they would have if they operated from the office.

As a remote manager, you have to be flexible, as distant communication will create a less formal interaction mode necessary to maintain engagement in a non-official environment. The first practical step to responding to a change in management style from physical to virtual is to have an orderly schedule that helps you coordinate your team and communicate with them frequently, collectively and individually to ensure every member performs their tasks.

You should also provide alternative communication methods for employees who may have challenges in using the chosen means of communication to avoid any feeling of exclusion. You should call your team members regularly to ensure they are stable and feel psychologically safe. You must establish ground rules to keep employees in check and discourage laziness that remote working might breed. Enforcing these changes is no easy task, but it will significantly enhance your management skill to a point where you can successfully lead a team to produce results regardless of circumstance and environment.

MANAGING YOUR TEAM REMOTELY

The coronavirus pandemic's onset has caused many organizations to adopt unconventional methods of management and running operations. Many businesses have suffered immensely due to revenue losses, stripped budgets, partial or full operations shut down, and staff layoffs. It has become glaring that a lot of face-to-face centric job descriptions can actually be performed remotely and still produce great results. There are so many handy virtual workspace tools that exist today which make performing tasks significantly easy. Thus, it is time to have a more digitized approach to completing assignments.

Managing a team remotely during the coronavirus pandemic places a tremendous demand for effective communication and feedback due to a lack of face-to-face supervision and interaction to measure employee engagement. It is necessary to develop remote work policies to ensure that team culture and standard operating procedures are maintained. To remotely manage a team, you must recognize its challenges and discern how to handle them so that you are not overwhelmed and lose control by allowing lapses in performance and a lack of team project engagement.

Earlier, when the lockdown restrictions started and companies had to adopt remote work, my team and I faced some challenges trying to work and collaborate in harmony. I recall our first struggle for scheduling a meeting on time that works for everyone in different time zones.

We achieved this by keeping our meetings short and straight to the point. Another major challenge was the differences in time zones. I needed to know the times when everyone was available and when our times overlapped. I discovered a few hours of overlap for some of us, and we worked out a way to collaborate. I had some of my virtual team in different time zones.

We had a few hours overlap between both teams. The team in time zone A was available from 12 pm to 3 pm, while the other team in time zone B was available from 9 am to 3 pm. In this way, we all worked collectively.

However, there are a lot of challenges that you can still face. They are:

Lapses in feedback

Feedback may not always come in real-time due to unforeseen circumstances instead of face-to-face communication in the office. Thus, progress on tasks may be slower, and it may affect team harmony.

Change is dynamic

Some individuals find it a lot easier to function optimally in a collaborative environment, which the office environment provides.

When working side-by-side with co-workers, it keeps morale high as there is a quick exchange of information. It is also easier to voice challenges and get help from co-workers when interacting physically. This factor may limit employee effectiveness in a remote environment.

Increase in stress levels

While remote working gives off a perception of comfort, in the real sense, it is not as easy as it seems because working under various personal circumstances can trigger an employee's stressors, which could affect performance. For instance, an employee with a family and kids will have to manage their family and contribute their quota to the team. It may affect their productivity level as the home may not necessarily offer an orderly and quiet atmosphere in the office space. Every employee cannot stifle all the external noise and work effectively in the face of many distractions.

Decreased sense of belonging

For employees that initially operated from the office environment, the transition from getting dressed up for the office every day to working at home could have adverse effects on their sense of belonging. An extended period away from their corporate family may cause a loss of the company culture's vision and goals.

Lack of access to resources

Most organizations were mostly unprepared for the changes which the covid-19 era brought; many employees whose tasks were more physical found it hard to work remotely. When an employee's job detail has to do with tangible resources, having to work with little or no access to their resources affects their output and may diminish their sense of duty.

As a manager, understanding these challenges is one thing, and effective tackling them is another. There are specific steps required for a manager to effectively take care of and get the best out of their remote team.

Regular communication with your team

Keeping regular communication with your team is an

essential part of managing them remotely. Working remotely may be a new concept for you and your team. So, you must understand there will be a learning curve - especially if your team isn't very tech-savvy.

One method to make this process easier is to have and show empathy for all employees. Always assure them that you are available to assist during the transition process and voice their concerns and questions. The pandemic era is stressful, and creating an open dialogue and showing some compassion will go a long way.

As a manager, another way you can also foster better communication is to encourage your employees to talk to their colleagues the same way they would if they were at the office.

The lack of human interaction has taken an unavoidable toll on people, but you can help employees feel more connected to each other while they are physically apart.

An excellent place to start is by saying "good morning" to one another and make time to chat over your morning coffee. It will help you and your team feel less remote.

Clearly outline work scope and expectations

Another necessary step to take when you remotely manage a team is to establish shared expectations with your group. These expectations cover everything from project scheduling, adjustments to production timeline charts, and virtual work hours.

Setting expectations is most effective through a conference call and should be reinforced through one-on-one conversations. In this way, every member clearly understands what is expected of them in the project.

When setting expectations, you must also consider how your team would respond and comply with them.

Therefore, you must Think Inclusively. If you're struggling to maintain the same performance levels now that you're working remotely, chances are your team members are too. So, let your remote situation influence the expectations of your group.

As a manager, you must also be Realistic. Over-the-top expectations will set you and your team up for failure. Certain project components may take a longer time to figure out. So, consider limiting project scopes until you are fully operational and comfortable with the remote setup.

It will significantly benefit your team if you provide documents or materials, they can reference to remind them of the project's expectations and changes. Video calls alone won't cut it.

Establish Team Norms

Most teams are not used to working remotely; it is a novel concept for some. Therefore, as a manager, it is necessary to discuss how you all plan to work together remotely with your team. A team comprises individuals with varied personalities and preferences. Thus, influential groups actively talk about their mutual expectations around topics like communication preferences, the timing of calls, discouraged behaviors, treatment of individuals, and how often meetings are organized. Therefore, as a manager, it is imperative to lay ground rules for effective remote management.

Here are a few ways to develop Team Norms.

Explain the relevance of team norms. Help your team understand the standards and why they are necessary. It might sound like this - **While working remotely, we must know how we will be most useful as a group. We may have all worked in ineffective groups and so are aware of behaviors that prompt such ineffectiveness. So, let us develop some ground rules that will guide us to work better.**

Ask each team member to propose a team norm. Team norms are most effective when they come from the team, not the leader. So, it is essential to involve your team when making these rules. You may ask each team member to propose a norm and pass it around until the team agrees on some. Also, the adoption of these norms should only occur if everyone in the group agrees.

It is also necessary to document team norms and post them virtually during meetings. Once the team has specific standards to guide them, display them during virtual meetings for easy reference.

- Here are some sample Team Norms;
- Limit virtual meetings to 45 minutes.
- Start and end meetings on time.
- No meetings on Thursdays.
- Anytime someone voices a concern, it should be heard and addressed. Employees should be encouraged to propose solutions.
- Quickly respond to team members' questions, and set the right expectations. Communicate, communicate, over-communicate.

Personally, as a team norm, I always ensure that during virtual meetings, team members have their video options turned on, so we can see one another's reactions to topics discussed.

Lead by example

As a manager leading your team remotely, you must walk your talk. You must be consistent in your actions and do what you say. If, for example, you schedule a meeting at 14:00, you must be ready to go at 13:45. You must also be proactive during virtual meetings and be a solution-provider.

Remote Employee Appreciation

Offering sincere appreciation to your team for specific work done right or just for their effort is an essential component of effective management. It is about human psychology. No one likes to feel unappreciated or work a thankless job. It may lead to resentment, apathy, and burnout. Conversely, a meaningful and sincere appreciation of an employee for their contributions has a far-reaching effect, including improving overall morale, work ethic, or company loyalty. As a manager, it is therefore essential to sincerely appreciate your team when they do things right.

Coaching through problems instead of micromanaging

A manager's role encompasses being a leader and a coach. Effective coaching fosters high employee performance and growth. However, coaching a team remotely may be daunting, and you may fall into the trap of micromanaging. It may be tempting to over-communicate with an employee you don't see in the office every day, perhaps just to let them know you still have them in mind - an admirable gesture indeed.

But as a manager, you must be aware that excessive

virtual hovering can foster insecurity and hinder engagement. This is particularly true for high-performing employees who have worked remotely in the past. For these people, constant check-ins can become distracting and insulting. Therefore, you must always endeavor to avoid micromanaging.

As a coach, you can always have a video conference, or travel to them, while being honest in your conversations. You should also consider using a supportive tone when communicating with your remote team.

Allowing flexibility for employees to work

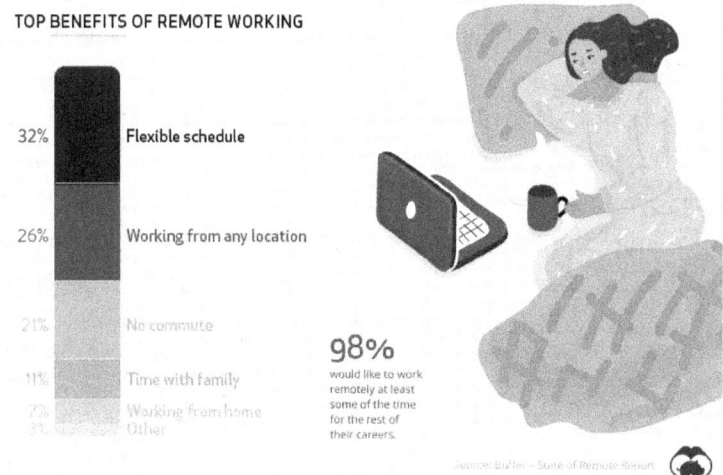

If there's anything the Coronavirus has introduced, it's the concept of flexibility in performing tasks. According to a study report by Buffer and AngelList, carried out on about 3500 remote workers worldwide, 32% of these workers prefer remote work because of the flexibility it affords, as shown in the graph above.

As a manager supervising a team remotely, I realized the importance of allowing employees to work and be productive where they are most comfortable to get the best out of their efforts. As a manager, you must understand each team member's strengths and leverage them towards achieving the team's objectives. Virtual workspaces like Slack and Trello are now popular mediums for collaboration. Some employees may prefer small physical co-workspaces. Whichever it is, as a manager, you should encourage flexibility for your teams in terms of working times and places.

Encourage employees to take risks and learn from them

As a manager, you should encourage, support, and even normalize risk-taking within your team. It is advisable to encourage your team to see every project as an experiment and success as the lab. So, they mustn't get the project right the first time. Changing your remote team's mindset to see failure as a learning process and diminishing its stigma is essential to them taking more risks. And so, words and messages are crucial. Virtual managers must frequently talk openly about risk-taking, what it is and means. Taking risks is something necessary to achieve our goals and gradually transforms us into someone very close to our ideal self. But doesn't the word "risk" immediately produce a great sense of fear for you? We are not used to taking risks. We avoid them and protect ourselves against them. It is completely normal. If we can, we always look for the easiest and safest way to achieve what we intend, but perhaps this is a sign of weakness? Wanting everything so easily is not good. The result will not be as satisfying.

"He who is not courageous enough to take risks will not achieve anything in life."

-Muhammad Ali

CHAPTER SUMMARY

We discussed that any manager's biggest challenge is effectively leading and coaching their team to be effective despite working remotely. A manager may face challenges such as:

- Poor communication due to distance and time zone differences.
- Employee effectiveness away from the office.
- You may have fewer resources to work with from home.
- You may need to be more hands-on and avoid micromanaging to get the best results from your team.
- You will need to establish effective ways to provide feedback to your team.

REFLECTIONS

Which quality of the best manager do you intend to improve on? What is your preferred management style?
Reflect:
_____

_____

_____

_____

How important feedback is for you? Do you have a process for mentoring your team members?
Reflect:
_____

_____

_____

_____

What are your most significant challenges in managing your team?
Reflect:
_____

_____

_____

_____

How has working remotely impacted the way you manage your team?
Reflect:
_____

_____

_____

_____

CHAPTER 4

WORK-LIFE BALANCE IS A HOAX

"You often feel tired, not because you've done too much, but because you've done too little of what sparks a light in you."

— **Alexander Den Heijer**

The term "work-life balance" has been in discussion for the past few years. This is partially due to the dominating presence of millennials in the workforce. Companies have been putting in tremendous efforts to determine the best ways to appeal to their millennial workforce. With this generation of workforce projected to take up to 75 percent of the workforce by 2025, many leaders think that it is time to redefine the concept of work-life balance.

It is an open secret that many people dread their jobs and only live for the paycheck. It is why most people feel so tired when they are at their workplaces and are all of a sudden energized when it is time to go home. Hence, many people love to hold onto the idea of a work-life balance. They always insist on a two-sided life that presents their work life and personal life differently.

They see themselves as two different entities. Their work personality is hardworking, having deadlines to meet, meetings to attend, and many more. Their personal life presents itself as a family person, taking the kids to school, spending time with their spouse, and meeting friends for drinks. I used to believe in this notion of work-life balance until I realized how miserable it made me feel and how much I struggled to create a balance that kept tumbling till it left me in a deep pool of frustration, anger, and resentment.

The work-life balance is a hoax, and ultimately, one needs to take proper control of their life. The first thing to always keep in mind is that we all have one experience. I always say there is no separation between your work life and your personal life. The anxieties, projects, family, friends, work, and many others are all thrown into one homogenous pool of stress.

The body, for example, is made up of different parts. These parts include the eyes, nose, mouth, head, legs, hands, ears, breasts, and many more. They are all housed together, and yet they perform different functions. Now I have never heard anyone describe their body as a two-way part. It is called a body, not two parts of a body. It shows that you only have one life and different parts that constitute life. You must learn how to attune these parts together to create a balance. In some ways, your body parts work together to assist you to carry out certain functions. If your hands were to start operating independently without control suddenly, I am pretty sure it would cause quite a shock. It is why you don't separate your life into parts.

I discovered the struggles attached to maintaining what I saw as the two sides of life - a liberating moment, I must say. During the early days of my career as a manager, I woke up every morning with a strong determination to maintain both lives. I even had a timetable in my head, where I assigned specific duties to certain times. For me, I was living a disciplined life until I discovered I was only running in circles. I'd become crankier, and executing my tasks seemed more like a chore. Instead of going about my duties with joy and a sense of freedom, I only looked forward to the closing hours of work. It was an endless loop of staleness for me, and I needed to fix it desperately. So, I started seeking ways to enjoy my job just as much as I enjoyed my time outside the office with family and friends.

To start my day with the right mindset, I adopted new rituals; I never snooze the alarm; snoozing the alarm meant breaking the promise I made to myself. Also, to clarify my thoughts, I don't check my phone first thing in the morning. It wasn't long before I was convinced that the concept of work-life balance is a hoax and that both sides of life are nothing but a poorly made-up idea deeply rooted in stressing you both emotionally and physically well.

There are no two sides to life. There is only one life. We all need to learn not to differentiate work from personal experience; instead, we should know to reconcile both sides of life. When we try to divide our lives into two unequal parts, it should come as no surprise when we continuously face challenges, which is the norm these days.

These challenges over time are bound to disrupt normal life processes, and as such, would put us in many difficult moments, which would not be easy to get out of eventually.

You must not see the work-life balance as a simple 9-5 work time frame or an hour-long commute to work. It is much more than this. The work-life balance is hard. No matter who you are, no matter the position you hold, no matter how long it takes you to commute to work, it does not matter. The more we believe that we have separate lives that we must navigate, instead of one experience that must be balanced, the more discouraged we become. We must change this mindset.

WORK LIFE BALANCE IS A HOAX

Some years ago, while I was struggling with my work-life balance. I was waking up as early as 5 a.m every day. As soon as I got up, I'd pace into the bathroom, take a quick shower, get dressed as quickly as possible, and jump into my car. In that period, my children barely saw me in the morning. I got to work before most of my team members, and I put up the essentials we needed for the day. By the close of work, I would sit in traffic for at least 30 minutes. On getting home, I'd commit some time to family bonding and then work on some files before bed. I thought I had it all figured out until I was facing my doctor behind a desk, and he let me know my lifestyle choice was slowly driving my health to the ground, and I needed to slow down.

That was an epiphany for me because I discovered work and life have no boundaries, and balance is dynamic, not static. Life itself is much more complicated than more work. Work-life balance is a complete fantasy, and believing in it is holding us back from true happiness. There is only one life, and you should balance it.

Learn to have a good rhythm of life, enjoy everything, including your work, life, family, friends, and more. This is my view on work-life balance. Many people tell me that they feel guilty when they spend more time at work and less time with their family. Ironically, these same people admit to also feeling guilty, not working when they are at home. The double dose of guilty is the perfect recipe for misery. I suggest that whenever you are working hard to meet a deadline, be realistic, understand that it's time to work. Once you are done with the project, make time to recharge, renew, and spend quality time with the people you love.

I am a staunch advocate of fully committing to

whatever you do. When you are working, fully commit to your work. When you are at home with your family or significant other, fully commit to engaging with them and enjoying your personal time. By understanding your rhythm, planning, and committing to the essential things in your life, you may not achieve perfection in balancing your life, but you will create a flow and rhythm that makes you happier, more productive, and erases guilt.

Most of the time, I observe that people face problems because they try to balance two things. Let's say you have your job, family, and friends in front of you. You are not trying only to balance it; you are also trying to optimize your life around it. The work-life balance is a myth and most people who fight hard to balance it fail because they view it as two different entities. Again, do well to remember that the work-life balance is one, and you need to enjoy yourself and optimize everything in your life.

We cannot ignore the impact of the Coronavirus pandemic; it came as a surprise and has outlasted experts' predictions. Every country in the world has felt its adverse effects. The pandemic has resulted in an economic recession in different nations, deaths of loved ones and friends, some persons have been relieved of their jobs, amidst a complete lockdown of many activities, including going to work. However, the pandemic has resulted in more creative ways for workers to carry out their duties.

Due to the pandemic, there is a surge in online meetings. Workers now sit in the comfort of their homes to work and engage in discussions. We can now tailor arrangements to suit everybody's needs as scheduled sessions are held at various times, and people can lie on their beds, join and contribute to discussions. It shows how much you can optimize life no matter the situation that may occur.

As a manager during the pandemic, I wake up to lazy mornings where I do my own thing at my own pace. Attend meetings scheduled for a few hours; still have more than enough time to catch up with family, social media, or my favorite shows. The new normal has afforded me some time to think deeper. Would the pandemic throw others who have struggled with the work-life balance into new ways of seeing work? Would they decide to change their mentality and opinions on the work-life balance? Would they strive to better their lives by merging into one experience? These questions and many more plagued my mind.

These changes have made me realize that life is indeed simpler when you know that the work-life balance that is fiercely discussed is the same whether you are on a 9-5 commute to work or are on your couch having an online meeting. I have been able to optimize my life in this pandemic. As a manager, I also remember that my team members look up to me, and I try to ensure that we are continually redefining how to deliver work and meet deadlines. Flexibility, open communication, and compassion have helped me keep my team on track to provide business and individual goals.

I also make sure my personal life is not lacking, and I perform my duties as a husband, father, son, and friend to my loved ones. I have one life and endeavor to balance it perfectly. People often blame different factors (work, company, boss) as the reason for their low work-life balance. One crucial lesson I have learned over time, which has helped me in planning, is; if you can't plan your work and life, it will not be balanced. For example, if you made no plans for retirement, you can't blame anyone when it beckons. Balance is vital in every aspect of our lives, and it requires conscious planning.

"When you love doing something, hard work is passion; otherwise, it gives you stress."

— Sharad Bajaj

I have also observed that most people end up in jobs they don't love, resulting in difficulties in creating a balance. And as such, they struggle tremendously and begin to see their life and work as two entities. Finding and getting a job you want means you don't have to work for the paycheck alone. You are merely working hard and seeing the progress, and nothing should bother you.

However, when you aren't doing what you love, you begin to lose focus, try too hard, and sometimes get fired because you lack the capabilities. It brings me to the point where I state that you should become a manager for the right reasons.

"Find a job you enjoy doing, and you will never have to work in your life."

— Mark Twain

As stated above, when you fully love and enjoy your work as a manager, finding a balance and realizing that there is only one side to life would come very quickly to you. I remember an incident that occurred before the pandemic started. I observed that a member of my team was looking more worn out as the days went by. I was, of course, bothered as this also affected their work input.

I did not make my concerns known initially, as I needed to be sure it wasn't a short time problem. However, a month into my observation, I decided to make a move. After our discussions, I discovered they were tired of the job, and they were struggling deeply with finding a balance. I gave my candid advice and told them to quit or do what makes them happy, or they needed to sit and learn that the work-life balance was an idea they needed to do away with after struggling for such a long time. I stated that they needed to change their mindset if they were having difficulties navigating work and personal affairs.

In no time, I saw an improvement. Not only did their work improve, but I also observed an absolute radiance from them. Their progress caused me to rethink several things, and I decided to hold a meeting to improve my team's well-being. I made sure to discuss the work-life balance properly, and it was an excellent interactive session.

The work-life balance is a myth you shouldn't indulge in. Always carry along with you a consciousness that recognizes both sides as one. When you make this recognition, you rest assured of a more comfortable life that lets you breathe and helps you optimize your experience at its best.

CHAPTER SUMMARY

As a manager and a human being, you have one life; find a balance. Find passion in your work and purpose in your life. The concept of work-life and personal life as different entities is a hoax. Do what you love, and you'll never dread the long hours.

REFLECTIONS

How do you ensure you have rhythm in your life?
Reflect:

How do you recognize when you're stressed? How do you help you team to handle stress?
Reflect:

What steps will you take to plan your work, life for the next three months?
Reflect:

CHAPTER 5

CULTURE – VALUES AND HABITS

"Culture eats strategy for breakfast." – **Peter Drucker**

Ok! you are now a manager heading a new department, and you tick all the managerial boxes in your organization. You seem to be settling into your new role, and so far, it's been fantastic! You are enjoying this new position and have never been happier working in your organization. However, you have left your old team and are set to manage a new and larger group.

You met a member of your new team yesterday, Mr. Wellington, whom you had asked to email a memo to the rest of the team for a brief team meeting in a few hours. However, it's been a couple of hours now, and you still haven't gotten any correspondence or acknowledgment on the proposed meeting. You refresh your work email, and there are still no new emails yet, which is unusual.

You feel a bit rattled and asked for Mr. Wellington to inquire about the proposed meeting; his reply was disappointing; he hadn't emailed the team at all. At this moment, you realized you needed to shake things up a bit.

Creating a defined, clear, and understandable culture in a team is vital as your group's quality and diverse expertise. Culture eats strategy for breakfast. If a team does not have a good culture, nothing will work. I always make sure that my team has an identity, a purpose, and a vision. To enforce these, I ensure that the team has a culture of winning and learning together. I have learned over the years that helping others creates an environment of value and capability. Talking through someone else's problems can give us the wisdom to tackle our challenges and motivate us to follow through.

Your team's purpose is about the direction your company wants to go, while values serve as a roadmap that will get you there. Habits, on the other hand, might be akin to the fitness regimen you undertake before a long hike or the car maintenance you do to make sure you don't break down on a road trip.

Values and habits together define a team's culture and make the idea of purpose, something that isn't just talked about in team meetings but is lived by your team every day. Leadership expert and author Anne Loehr says,

"Purpose is the middle of the compass. It's the arrow pointing to our true north; our values are NSWE. Values tell us how we will achieve our purpose. They guide us and tell us how to make decisions. Purpose and values together increase engagement, someone's willingness to make a strong contribution to work."

YOUR ROLE IN BUILDING CULTURE

Good managers build good teams; great managers foster the right culture. When you promote the right culture in the group, you create a practice or a set of guidelines that characterizes the business and announces what it stands for; it is essentially a company's value system, which is developed and enforced by the executive tier of the company and sustained over time.

It often forms the framework with which companies develop Best Practice Models. Just as there are different cultures in society, various organizations have distinctive cultures that separate one. As such, an organization's culture must be clear, precise, and long-lasting, without which the structure of a company stands the risk of falling apart.

Organizational culture

Organizational culture is the value system that governs and characterizes a team's behavior or an organization from the top to the very bottom of the corporate chain.
Culture is the soul of a team; it guides a team's operations. In any challenging situation, the team can fall back on their values and culture. A team should live and breathe their culture.

The management often establishes this value system and duly passes it down to various groups and departments using practical communication tools to ensure proper understanding. Successful communication of these values is when employees embody the company's values.

The essence of a healthy organizational culture must be understood alongside the consequences of the absence thereof, as it primarily affects an organization's social and psychological atmosphere.

The essence of culture is to construct an effective response towards various workplace situations and devise a proper line of action in the discharge of duties. Put, culture affects the workforce's overall output and, thus, the success of an organization. As a manager, building and sustaining a winning culture is imperative, and I always strive to establish it in my team. When there is a defined culture in a group, the chances for success become significantly higher because every person knows their tasks and performs them efficiently.

Importance of Right Culture

These are some observable benefits of having the right culture in a team:

- Encourages team spirit.
- Provides a guiding principle to the team.
- Serves as a troubleshooting guide.
- Ensures dynamism
- Serves as a useful guide for day-to-day.
- Enhances productivity and output.
- Promotes positivity and a sense of belonging.
- Ensures uniformity
- Promotes effective communication.

Encourages team spirit

Individuals within a team are more likely to cooperate and perform optimally in a project when they share the same values. They can discharge their assigned tasks using a common viewpoint, and this also affects how they relate to one another as culture greatly influences behavior in the workplace.

Serves as a troubleshooting guide

To a considerable extent, culture affects and shapes employees' attitudes towards work and clients; hence, it determines their response to various organizational situations.

Increases team's efficiency

There are many matrices to measure team performance in the workplace, and culture is one of them. It helps highlight individuals that represent the core values of an organization. Such people need to be identified and groomed for leadership succession.

Ensures dynamism

In a fast-paced and rapidly evolving society such as this, a strong culture serves as the driving force behind an organization that motivates a team despite the changes going on around them; every team must be progressive not to lose the vision and become disorganized.

Serves as a useful guide for day-to-day

There are higher rates of successful hires when a defined company culture is tedious to assess a potential employee's suitability. It is much more comfortable and efficient to successfully onboard candidates using the same already established culture.

Enhances productivity and output

The productivity of employees in an organization has a direct link with their level of job satisfaction. The overall satisfaction of employees (whether physical or psychological) will reflect on their output level.

Source: Field Data, 2015

The graph above shows the different levels of satisfaction and the performance rate of employees. You can see that when employees are very much satisfied, their performance rates increase. Conversely, a very dissatisfied group, will have a low productivity level.

There is an inextricable link between an organization's culture and its employees' performances, and it is essential to note that culture does not end in aspiration. It must be acted upon and continually practiced taking the course to ensure the business's exponential growth.

Promotes positivity and a sense of belonging

It is your duty as a manager to relate effectively and communicate with your team to understand that they are a part of something grand. It shapes a positive outlook of staff towards the organization, thus giving them a sense of belonging.

Ensures uniformity

A well-structured organization must conform to a routine method of carrying out its functions. Its culture helps teams comply with a standard operating procedure to achieve order and unison.

Promotes effective communication

Besides shaping employees' corporate values, the culture encourages proper communication between team members and, most notably, between employee and client to ensure excellent customer experience, which leaves the client with a positive image of the brand.

Conversely, some consequences of low organizational culture include the following:
- Decline in overall performance and revenue
- Increased turnover
- Increased cost of new-hires
- Poor customer experience

Decline in overall performance and revenue

I often study companies that I feel have an impeccable work culture. I immediately take note of where they are, how much they have grown within a given time to gauge their overall success with their culture, and I also study failing companies on the verge of collapse.

I try to figure out the lapses they permitted to have gotten to that point. I have realized that company performance is inextricably linked to a given culture's perpetuation, whether positive or detrimental.

Increased turnover

When an organization's leadership fails to communicate the established culture to the team correctly, it leads to unmotivated individuals who do not see the bigger picture. It often creates a divide and breeds the spread of its negative views and a lackadaisical attitude towards work; such detachment could encourage staff resignation.

When several employees leave the organization simultaneously, this can significantly affect workflow due to excess workload, thus going to the team to pick up the slack, which can be overwhelming and could cause disorganization of the work process.

The increased cost of new-hires

A high turnover creates an opportunity for more hires for business processes to flow swiftly; this leads to the disbursement of "un-budgeted" resources needed to source for impromptu engagements.

Poor customer experience

A toxic culture will reflect how employees interact with a client, which leaves the client with a tainted image of the organization due to poor customer experience. If such a culture is not curbed, it could harm an organization's growth.

BUILD A MEANINGFUL ORGANIZATIONAL CULTURE

The best employees see value in their work; they wake up in the morning and do not cringe at the thought of going to the office to carry out their tasks. Instead, they look forward to it and anticipate an opportunity to work with their corporate family and contribute a meaningful quota to achieve the set milestones.

An employee develops such an attitude towards work when they feel a sense of belonging, from a healthy organizational culture. Thus, these employees may be referred to as "drivers," as they are forged primarily through following the step-by-step process of building an influential workplace culture.

Having an entire team of drivers will contribute significantly to the bottom line of any organization. Let us take an intensive look at some of these practical steps:

1. **Identify purpose in deciding on a culture that fits**

A culture without solid principles will quickly crash, so do not be in a hurry to throw it all into the pot because it looks good. If it carries no real value, then it defeats the purpose of why it needs to be in the first place. At the same time, the cost of building an influential workplace culture is relative to a given organization; it requires time and strategy to establish.

Therefore, a manager must take the time to create a workplace culture that will reflect the company's values and will stand the test of time. You must envision where you want the company to be in the next ten years relative to its present state. Your culture must be futuristic yet cater to the now, while the company's purpose and future are in view. You must take into account the end and purpose of your workforce as well, and your team should be on the same level of growth and progress as the company. When you achieve this, you are on the right track; hence your culture should be one that guarantees all-round development.

2. Set clear goals

Behind every culture lies an objective; you must set clear and workable goals for your team that align with your organizational culture. Your team's involvement in this process is essential because they will be the engine that drives the vehicle of success.

At the same time, you supply the fuel. One cannot work without the other. You must lay your goals out openly before your team to identify whatever challenge or concerns they may have regarding attaining the purpose to guide them through it as best you can and provide whatever incentive or tools needed to aid them in the overall process.

3. Lead with Examples

It begins with you successfully selling an idea to a team of individuals with individual mindsets and viewpoints. You must first show them practically how and why it works; the image is not to impose a culture on your team but to give them an exact reason as to why they should carry it on. It invariably means that you must be the poster person in the picture you are trying to paint.

This factor differentiates a 'figurehead' from a leader as a leader practices what he teaches. In contrast, a figurehead gives the orders and sits back in his high chair, waiting to see his orders carried out.

4. Encourage Team Building

A healthy relationship between team members is imperative for the stability and essential to the continuity of workplace culture. Companies with a workforce so diverse that members of the same group may not even know each other.

The only chance they get to be acquainted or see one another is during a general meeting or briefing; this should not be the norm.

There should be healthy codependency between co-workers; the significance of a tight-knit work relationship is to create room for partnership and cooperation, which is an intricate part of an organization's culture.

Therefore, an excellent way to achieve this is to take up team building exercises geared towards breaking the ice within your team.

Great examples are games such as scavenger hunts and puzzle games, which can be performed during office breaks or outside the office in the form of team excursions and team-building workshops.

Adopting these techniques helps establish a strong bond within a team and improve your team's dynamic.

5. Offering rewards & incentives

As a leader, you must be a motivator. One way to spur your team on is to appreciate them for their efforts, especially when exemplary; this helps boost team morale and inspires hard work. You must identify your team members' needs and interests and offer them incentives for a great display or practice of the established culture.

6. Apply active listening technique

Listening is a soft skill that every leader must have to induce a new culture into their daily work lives successfully. Listening skills can be beneficial during one-on-one sessions with individuals in your team.

As a manager, your communication style will eventually prove to be mostly inefficient if you are the only one who speaks during team meetings; sometimes, you have to listen a lot more than you talk.

Listening requires you to grant an audience to an individual without interrupting them and offer your transparent and honest feedback when the individual has finished speaking.

You should be able to identify keynotes of what has been communicated and reflect on them without judgment. A successful interaction should leave the door open for the individual to return and seek counsel whenever they encounter a challenge.

In applying these six steps, it is essential to note that none carries more significant importance than the other, but instead, they are all linked and work together to produce results.

Therefore, none should be skipped but applied appropriately in their respective stages to ensure success.

TRANSPARENCY, OPENNESS, IDENTITY

"A team is a collection of people with a shared identity who collaborate to achieve a common mission."
- Adam Grant

One of the effective ways to harness team identity is to ask your team to come up with a name that identifies the group collectively. This technique is prevalent in the military and special forces. A team's name gives its members a clear identity and purpose, and each team member understands the meaning. The term 'ninja" is a favorite pick that I always opt for in my teams. Autonomy and psychological safety go hand-in-hand and are essential traits of successful teams. Teams with freedom and flexibility become more creative and innovative; they feel safer to take risks and speak up in their team. Leaders should actively work to ensure all members feel a strong sense of team identity.

Clear team identity and purpose give a group a reason to work on a project day after day until they achieve their goals. The purpose of undertaking an action will always be ahead of more relevance than the need for said action. As a leader, you must ensure that team members know and connect to work on a project rather than for a project. There is a vast difference in the performances of those who work for a paycheck and those who work for a purpose.

"In the chase between the lion and the deer, many times the deer wins because while the lion runs for food, the deer runs for its life."

The above quote typifies the essence of purpose. One way to accomplish a sense of purpose is by letting every team member know each individual's roles on the team to see the responsibility. How does everyone contribute? What does their workload look like? Then, back this up by ensuring everyone knows their job has meaning and that what they are doing is valuable. Doing so leads to a 93% increase in the odds of psychological safety. When teams prioritize work and tackle projects together, they strengthen collaboration, purpose, and belonging. It contributes to an 88% increase in the odds of having a psychologically safe culture.

Finally, after every project, hold an honest review all together to experience success and failure as a team, not individually, so everyone feels accountable, and no one is singled out. The team should be willing to give and receive honest, critical feedback to make the team stronger. When these things are done, there is a 55% to 91% increase in the odds of psychological safety, respectively. "Teamwork begins by building trust with each other."

DIVERSITY, INCLUSION, AND BELONGING (DIB)

"Diversity is having a seat at the table, Inclusion is having a voice, and belonging is having that voice heard."

- Liz Fosslien

Diversity constitutes the differences that exist among individuals in an organization. Inclusion deals with how those differences influence an employee's experience within the organization. And, belonging is a feeling of being rightly placed within the organization.

The most crucial aspect to be considered when building a diverse work environment is creating an environment where your employees feel safe and confident enough to be their authentic selves and can offer ideas, innovation, and experience. Therefore, there is a need to show diverse individuals that they are valued and fit perfectly into a given organization's structure.

Diversity, Inclusion, and Belonging (DIB) are the foundation of the ideal 'employee experience,' affecting the employee's overall performance. Diversity and inclusion will win the skill and expertise of an employee.

However, belonging will win you their passion; this is to say that diversity and inclusion alone aren't where they end; facilitating a sense of belonging is needful to build a resilient and loyal team.

There will always be different characteristics among individuals in the workplace, but how these all come to play will influence how welcome and included they feel in a corporate environment. Navigating through these factors as a leader will test your ability to manage people and situations.

DIVERSITY

"Strength lies in difference, not in similarities."

- Stephen Covey

Every organization must strive to have diverse employees. It is essential to balance how they all manifest in the workplace as it reflects productivity. I have observed that companies with a more diverse workforce are high performers.

Therefore, diversity is crucial. It gives an organization a competitive advantage over others in employing talents from different backgrounds, perspectives, ages, and genders, which creates a whirlpool of ideas for the company.

The new age we exist in has heralded diversity in various workplace forms; whether it is gender diversity, age, demographic, religion, race, and personality, you name it! Organizations are beginning to show more representation in their selection of employees as it dramatically affects their output and speaks volumes about their organizational culture.

Diversity plays a vital role in individual interactions and performances in the workplace, as their differences often inform their thought process.

Creating a common ground is essential to establishing a healthy workplace dynamic. A diverse workforce is critical to any organization's growth. These different backgrounds and experiences offer a supply of fresh ideas that carry the potential for innovation that could contribute to its development.

As a manager, you must devise a means to harness and manage a diverse team to bring out everyone's best. An imbalance in diversity could cause disarray and disrupt the harmony of your workplace. Diversity is more than just a moral responsibility.

It's foundation to the success of your team. When building team, you should not just assign tasks—you should frame your approach to the problem. Each team member brings their unique perspective and expertise to the team, widening the range of possible outcomes. If you want a breakthrough idea, you're more likely to get it with a diverse team.

Remember, diverse teams see the same problem from many angles. They have a better understanding of any given situation and generate more ideas, making them more effective problem solvers. It takes effort to harness and align different perspectives, but it is the source of our most meaningful breakthroughs.

INCLUSION

To make an employee feel included, you need to take some time to study and understand what makes them unique and then know how to strategically place such individuals to enable them to thrive in the work environment and express themselves professionally. One of the significant ways to achieve this is to address an employee on a first-name basis. It shows that you recognize their individuality.

This is possible, no matter how large your team or workforce is. As long as you engage your team members individually regularly, seek their input in meetings instead of being the only one to share ideas during group discussions. There is a need for you to show leadership and sensitivity towards your team members to guide them into becoming a part of a professional community.

An exciting way to boost inclusion is to set up events or an avenue where each employee represents and showcases their cultural heritage and celebrates with the team.

In my group, we often hold potlucks to celebrate the diverse festivals of different cultures, which helps many people learn about different foods and drinks from other cultures. Such exercises go a long way in engaging various employees and educating others about each other's background to boost effective communication amongst co-workers in the work environment.

I first experienced this concept when I worked in a company where there was usually a cultural day on the last Friday of every month when every employee had to come to work dressed in their cultural attire.

I observed that this fostered a healthy relationship between co-workers, where they would interact with one another with keen interest as they tried to learn more about each other's culture based on their clothing. It led to many shared experiences and information about cultural backgrounds as they told one another stories about where they are from, which helped create a better bond between staff.

BELONGING

"Diversity is a fact; inclusion is a behavior, but belonging is the emotional outcome people want in an organization"

– Christianne Garofalo

On the topic of diversity and inclusion, we often fail to recognize that just because someone is included in our organization doesn't mean that they feel a sense of belonging. Everyone can think of a moment when they felt like they didn't belong. It's not a feeling you forget in a hurry because it hurts.

Belonging is a feeling, and therefore is a far more powerful force than any diversity and inclusion strategy could ever be. It is a fundamental human need, a word that translates across any language or culture, and a feeling that every human is wired to want.

It is why most individuals either belong to some social, religious, or community group or the other, and this trait extends to their corporate environment.

An individual that feels like an essential part of an organization will put their energy into making it better; this is how the employee transitions from a worker into a brand advocate, at what point he lives and breathes the organization and extends his representation of the company beyond the confines of the workspace, this is the kind of attitude you must strive to foster as a leader, as having an entire team of brand advocates will significantly introduce a steady wave of progress within your organization.

A keen sense of belonging is a better motivator than a monthly salary; this theory is correct when there is a slight delay in payment of wages. You may observe that some employees begin to loaf around and relax when performing their duties, but this is not so when an employee feels a sense of belonging; they remain dedicated even in the face of such setbacks.

Belonging is The Gateway to innovation for businesses today. Design is fundamental and imperative for any company. Diverse perspectives, new ideas, creativity, and risk-taking are the superpowers every company tries to attain. However, few have realized that their kryptonite has employees who don't feel like they belong.

Many companies seek a more diverse workforce as it offers unique talents and attributes. Organizational diversity also improves decision-making and affects output and revenue.

For instance, if a company that generally manufactures men's products decides to make women's products, there will automatically require more gender diversity in the organization.

Therefore, female employees are essential to offer a fresh perspective on what works best for women. Also, how best to showcase feminine products in a way that is appealing to its target market; this would, in turn, improve performance and show better results compared to having only men on the team making these decisions.

However, diversity encompasses different elements that are not just limited to gender or ethnicity; it also covers marital status, age, sexuality, disability, political orientation, genetic information, religious affiliations, and a lot more.

Thus, there is a need for some level of strategy in deciding what form of diversity would best suit your organization, trigger growth, and boost its image. A healthy work environment should breed acceptance, more so when there is diversity, minorities should have equal rights and enjoy similar benefits as every other employee.

Although diversity and inclusion are separate concepts, they are closely linked because inclusion measures the extent to which efforts to induce variety may succeed. Without inclusion, a diverse workforce can quickly become toxic, as there will be more focus on differences than uniqueness, which could cause conflict, distrust, and intolerance.

Employees need to recognize and appreciate individual uniqueness to have a balanced and healthy relationship with one another in the organization. Hence, both factors are essential to encourage belonging.

As a leader, you must understand the need for every individual voice to be heard and promote equality by granting equal access to your team's resources to propel their growth. You must always strive to break the ice in your team and allow a free communication flow if you hope to see excellent results in performances.

It is up to you to create a safe and comfortable environment for individuals to thrive and to foster cooperation in your team.

PSYCHOLOGICAL SAFETY

"When a team fears punishment, they focus on consequences, which is the wrong value. Fear of punishment diminishes self-esteem and goodwill."

- **Sharad Bajaj**

It is impossible to fully understand the importance of maintaining a psychologically safe culture without a firm grasp on what psychological safety truly means. It is the freedom to apply yourself by offering your ideas and skill without harboring a fear of receiving backlash that could reflect poorly on your self-image. A psychologically safe culture leaves room for an employee to take calculated risks without being attacked in a way that will damage self-esteem, diminish their confidence in their abilities or make the individual feel like their input is not welcome.

It creates an environment where members within a team can respect each other's points of view and be more accepting as they share ideas. It does not allow any form of marginalization in the way employees relate to one another.

Thus, an employee who feels safe can express themselves and share their perspective to promote growth and achieve an objective. A winning team is a team of risk-takers forged by a strong, psychologically safe culture.

Psychological safety is a state of mind that believes one will not be punished for speaking up about concerns or mistakes. It is a topic that should never be overlooked in the workplace as it dramatically affects the mental and emotional conditioning of employees. It determines the quality of their output; just as there is a physical interaction between employees and their corporate environment, there is also a psychological interaction.

So, a manager should closely monitor psychological conditions so as not to create a toxic work environment. A psychologically safe culture is one that does not breed antagonism, fear, or anxiety.

An institution is psychologically safe when it does not permit any form of attack or manipulation on its employees' psychological state and provides a safe learning environment where mistakes are adequately handled by offering proper guidance and encouragement to improve upon areas of weakness. Sometimes, as an employee, you might have charming colleagues, who ask about your weekend, remember their birthday, and even invite you for happy hours. However, you may still find it challenging to speak up at meetings. Perhaps, you are nervous, afraid to look inferior or have a close-minded manager who is opposed to new ideas. So, you figure, what's the point?

When someone makes a mistake, I examine the negative behavior as an observation and ask them to explain the reason for their action. For instance, I might say, "I noticed you haven't been hitting your deadlines over the past few months. I assume some factors are limiting your ability to get your work done. Can you walk me through what these factors are?"

Additionally, I don't spend too much time on fault-finding - instead, I focus on solutions. I would say something like, "I'd like to brainstorm a few solutions with you if that's okay. How can I best support you? In the end, leaders focus on what is right, not who is right.

Good leaders and managers learn to operate outside their views and work with the point of view of their team. They put their team's needs ahead of personal needs.

Employees come to work with various states of mind based on their interactions and experiences within their environment outside the workplace. Simultaneously, some may have the ability to unpack whatever negative mindsets they may have developed due to these interactions.

Others may not, which can change their attitude towards co-workers and how they perform their tasks. Part of my daily office routine as a manager is to start my team off with laughter at the end of the team briefings. I like to tell a joke or engage them in a riddle before sending them off to their various workspaces.

I do this to lighten their mood and have them start their tasks in an upbeat mood to change a gloomy countenance and counteract whatever negative emotions they may be harboring within themselves that could jeopardize the objectives of the day. From my experience, an employee will never speak up at meetings if they feel everyone else in the room is perfect. By admitting to my mistakes, I am creating space for others to do the same.

Even though you leave the door open for your employees to approach you and speak to you about their challenges, there are specific issues they may not be so forward about that could seriously affect their work dynamic. Such matters are mostly personal. Therefore, as part of promoting a safe psychological culture, you must think outside the box regarding balancing their psychological state. It is vital because there are many psychological issues that an employee may be dealing with within the workplace, such as depression, anger, fear, and anxiety. As a manager, you must take smart steps to check and remediate any form of psychological distress among individuals in your workplace as it can significantly affect their performances. An unhappy employee is likely to lash out at their colleagues and spread the gloom.

You should know that not every idea is good, and many of times, there are stupid questions being asked in the meeting, and yes disagreements can slow things down, but talking through these things is an essential part of the creative process.

People must be allowed to voice half-finished thoughts, ask questions, and brainstorm out loud; it creates a culture in which a minor miss or momentary lapse is no big deal, and where actual mistakes are owned and corrected, and where the next left-field idea could be the next big thing.

Consequently, you no longer have one moody employee; you have a handful of unhappy employees who will either choose to shut down or produce haphazard work due to an unclear state of mind.

A depressed employee will likely have a lackadaisical attitude towards work. Those who suffer from anxiety will continually relegate themselves to the background and avoid making contributions or getting involved in team activities.

These negative emotions play a significant role in destabilizing teams and can affect organizational growth if left unaddressed. Some companies overcome this by having a guidance counselor within the office who can help co-workers work through their difficulties as it affects their ability to function in the workplace. Nobody wishes to leave part of their personality and life at home.

We all wish to be fully present at work and feel "psychologically safe." To achieve this, we must know that we have the freedom to share our concerns without fear of recriminations. We must have difficult conversations with colleagues who are driving us insane.

I often recalled some years ago, my team and I had to build a new product within a short deadline. One of the ground rules for all the teams I've managed is "quality over speed," However, this project needed us to work fast, which inevitably impacted its quality. I assumed everyone in the team didn't mind the trade-off.

During our one-on-one session, I later discovered that a team member was not in support of my suggestion of delivering fast work over quality work because that wasn't part of the team's culture.

What shocked me was that this individual did not feel psychologically safe enough to air their views to me for fear of punishment.

I had to immediately address the team on the need to always share their opinions even if it contradicts everyone else's and feel safe.

BENEFITS OF A PSYCHOLOGICALLY SAFE CULTURE

Organizations must indeed focus on performance. However, the challenge is ensuring a balance between learning and efficient performance from employees. A useful model to ascertain how an organization functions is a 2 x 2 matrix. On one axis, there's performance pressure (accountable results). On the other axis, there is psychological safety.

Here's a pictorial representation between psychological safety and performance level from p2theblog.

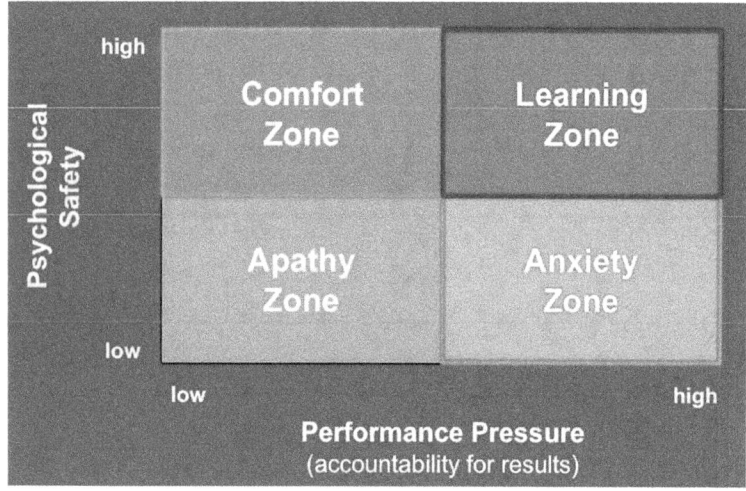

From the above diagram, when psychological safety and accountability levels are low (apathy zone), the team is apathetic and always maneuver for positions. This is mostly typified in bureaucratic organizations, where seeking favor rather than sharing ideas is a norm.

When there's no psychological safety, but accountability levels are high (anxiety zone), employees get anxious and stressed. They become cautious about offering new ideas, airing their opinions, taking risks because they fear the consequences. Burnout typifies these types of organizations.

In organizations that encourage high psychological safety levels but low-performance levels (comfort zone), complacency is inevitable. Employees have the notion that doing the bare minimum is the norm.

When psychological safety and performance pressures go hand in hand (learning zone), then there is an ideal environment for employees to grow and give their best efforts to the organization.

The extent to which psychological safety improves the synergy in an organization is boundless. It touches every workforce tier, from the executives to managers, team leads, and team members. The following are somehow promoting a psychologically safe culture could be beneficial to an organization:

- Individuals are not afraid to take calculated risks.
- It helps maintain a sense of purpose and belonging amongst employees.
- It promotes team effectiveness.
- It creates a supportive environment among employees.
- It fosters effective communication.
- Provides a safe learning environment
- It rules out marginalization.
- It promotes inclusion
- It promotes healthy competition.
- It encourages the high engagement of employees.
- It promotes participative management.

- It guarantees innovation
- It promotes a better relationship between individuals of different ranking.

To cultivate a psychologically safe environment as a leader, you must check and balance some essential elements to make sure there is no threat to the identity of any member of your team. As such, you have to make changes in your approach towards addressing your team members and educate them on how to handle themselves to make one another feel secure around each other.

You must avoid certain words or remarks which are invasive. Refrain from using abusive languages when correcting an individual.

You must take care to use the proper tone instead of yelling as this could dampen their morale and render excellent feedback ineffective. You should never ridicule an individual during the process of correcting them. Ask for employee feedback, and remain thankful for any feedback you receive.

One of the easiest ways to create a psychologically safe environment is to ask your employees what you can do better to support them or make them more open to sharing ideas and opinions.

But if you shut them down when they try to give feedback, it will hinder you from creating a psychologically safe space.

Instead, take their input seriously, act on it, and consider strategies that might strengthen your leadership skills for the team. And, always say, "thank you for your valuable feedback; I really appreciate it.". Many leaders don't know that feedback is a gift, it comes in many shapes and colors.

Some managers use threats to keep their team grounded, but this is negative and robs the group of security in the workplace.

In addressing and correcting a mistake made by an employee, you must leave them feeling empowered rather than depreciated.

MINDSET

"Thoughts are behaviors we haven't learned to observe yet."

- B.F Skinner.

Mindset is a belief that informs the way we handle situations. It is a mental disposition or a frame of mind. Your mindset is your collection of thoughts and opinions that shape your thought habits. And your thought habits affect how you think, what you feel, and what you do.

Have you noticed that why is it that some people seem to shine in any sphere in which they choose to exert themselves, and others cannot manage even a glimmer despite having obvious talent? The answer to this question is rooted in mindset, it's all about how they think about their ability that really counts.

Most of those who have achieved greatness, have worked extremely hard to get there. Many were told that they would never amount to anything. But they believed that they could achieve, and worked hard to do so.

As a manager, it is a constant challenge to keep your team with the right mindset. Improving each team member's attitude can make a huge difference in achieving success in a group. For example, I believe that cleaning is a mindset or habit, and so it shouldn't be a task.

Similarly, if you want your team to deliver excellent work, you must ensure excellence is something the group chases individually and collectively.

For example, let's say that you are alone and walking into a clothing store and accidentally knocked down a stack of jeans from a rack; the natural action to take is placing it right back where it was, even if no one noticed what happened. If you foster a culture where each team member's mindset is aligned with the principles of success, you will get the desired results. There is no doubt that the process will be daunting and would require constant improvement. So, as a manager, you must be relentless in your pursuit of building the right mindset in your team.

GROWTH MINDSET

Carol Dweck, an American researcher, coined the term. It explains the fluidity and malleability of the human potential, skill, and ability through training, mentorship, and passion for achieving progressive success.

The growth mindset believes that you can harness and develop your inherent qualities to achieve higher personal or professional success levels. It is a concept that shows that a person or a people can progressively move from one stage of accomplishment to another; it recognizes a chance to improve on areas of weakness to gain ground and overtake one's counterparts. There is either a growth mindset or a fixed mindset.

The latter tends more towards the extremes of possibility or impossibility and is most restrictive. Thus, it leaves very little room for taking risks that brings you a step closer to achieving your goals. It is highly limiting compared to the growth mindset, which welcomes challenges that trigger exponential growth by embracing a chance for development at every conceivable stage.

A growth mindset is a significant factor that determines the future of any organization. You cannot achieve growth in a company where employees are stagnant, and a company's development is proportional to its workforce's growth mindset.

Where the fixed mindset says "not possible," the growth mindset says "not yet." The growth mindset keeps you motivated in a highly competitive and continuously evolving atmosphere.

If a company is not always making moves to get to a higher level by taking calculated risks, it will remain at the bottom. A well-functioning company should not stay in the same position for too long; in the space of 5 years, a healthy organization should experience multiple levels of growth.

You must have heard someone sharing their experience and inspiring you to make an effort to enhance your abilities. If you feel the urge of doing it by making efforts, then you certainly possess a growth mindset.

In my personal experience, people with a fixed mindset, their brain is most active when they are being given information about how well they have done, for example, finishing up an important milestone of a project.

Whereas, people with a growth mindset, their brain is most active when they are being told what they could do to improve.

HOW GROWTH MINDSET AFFECTS AN EMPLOYEE

It is crucial to have a growth mindset because skills are no longer rigid these days; they are continually upgrading as time progresses to accommodate versatility. Therefore, the need to develop one's skills is getting increasingly essential in the workplace. If you are the only team member who refuses to evolve, you will quickly become a risk and potentially slow down the group's progress.

Thus, you move a step closer to being disengaged from the company based on an inability to keep up with its progressive pace. Nowadays, companies invest considerably in training and developing their employees' skill sets to support the next growth phase.

The passion for stretching yourself and sticking to it, especially when it's not going as planned, is a sign of the growth mindset. It is this mindset that makes you thrive during some of the most challenging times of your life. Here are some specific and practical examples of how you can apply the growth mindset in your job:

1. Do not feel offended by criticism from a manager. Instead, use the feedback to get better at your job.
2. You may need to complete a task that's new to you, which can breed insecurity. In this instance, do not think, "I will never succeed," but be confident that you will learn the new skills that you will need.
3. If you are a manager, opt for task rotation or even job rotation. That way, your employees will continue to develop their skill sets.
4. When hiring new staff, pay attention to their abilities to learn something new.

5. See new tasks, actions, tactics, and strategies as experiments leading to new insights, rather than activities that must lead to success.

An individual with a growth mindset concentrates on their tasks to get to where they envision. Having a growth mindset makes you a forward thinker with a can-do attitude, and you are not easily discouraged when you face difficulty in accomplishing your tasks. Instead, you go back to your drawing board to figure out where you went wrong, implement corrective measures, and try again. An employee with a fixed mindset in a company that believes in growth will quickly fade out of the larger picture.

HOW THE GROWTH MINDSET AFFECTS A MANAGER

"The moment that we believe that success is determined by an ingrained level of ability, we will be brittle in the face of adversity"

-Josh Waitzkin

Remember the story of the tortoise and the rabbit? The rabbit was so certain that he would win the race so he sat down and went to sleep during the race. The tortoise just plodded on and kept going, always thinking that he had a chance of winning. When the rabbit woke, he started running as fast as he could, but he was just too late: the tortoise had won.

The rabbit had a fixed mindset. He believed that his innate ability would always mean that he would win whatever he did.

The tortoise had a growth mindset. He believed that he needed to work hard and keep going if he was to win. He was also not afraid of failure or he would never have agreed to race the rabbit.

As a manager, you play a crucial role in determining the level of growth your team or company achieves and maintains. As such, you need to continually demonstrate the growth mindset to condition your team to contribute passionately to your company's growth. Hence, you need to monitor your team keenly to know their development levels, which you can achieve through interaction and active communication with them. You can identify the skills and critical competencies that are missing but needed to complete the next milestone, which is instrumental in driving its growth plan.

You must also make sure to shut down any attitude within your team that shows a fixed mindset by making them understand that whatever they are unable to do now, they can do excellently tomorrow through proper guidance.

One trait that every successful team has is growth mindset; you need to get your team to have a positive outlook towards projects, especially challenging ones. Even when you fail to achieve a goal, you need to maintain team morale by recognizing that failure is not a dead-end but an opportunity to do things differently and produce even better results a second time. A manager with a fixed mindset puts the entire organization's future at risk and induces a thick atmosphere, which could be very discouraging to your team members.

The fixed mindset believes that skills are innate and set-in-stone and that successful people are born to be successful. Failure (and trying) is feared and avoided because it would be a public confirmation of a lack of ability.

The growth mindset accepts that success is simply the outcome of learning, but most importantly, failure IS learning, which is the way to success. The growth mindset embraces failure and isn't afraid to take up new challenges.

In an organizational culture, the fixed mindset manifests as a fear of failure. If something doesn't work, it must be the fault of someone who isn't good enough, and so, these people should be weeded out.

Everything then becomes "spin" and fake success. In this environment, nobody learns anything.

The growth mindset embraces experimentation and failure as the keys to growth. Failed experiments are seen as more valuable than successful ones because they provide more learning potential.

Do you know that lions only succeed in a quarter of their hunting attempts? This means that 75 percent of their endeavors are futile, and only 25 percent are a success. Despite this small margin, they do not despair in their pursuit.

The primary reason for this isn't the hunger they feel, as some might presume, but it is the understanding of the "Law of Wasted Efforts" that is instinctively built into animals, a law that governs nature.

Only humans see the lack of success after many attempts as a failure, but the truth is that we only fail when we "stop trying." Success isn't having a life devoid of pitfalls; it is learning from your mistakes, going beyond every stage of wasted efforts, and looking forward with optimism.

The following are a few indicators that I use every so often to measure my team's mindset index:
- Does my team proactively seek opportunities to improve service delivery/results/outcomes?

- Do they demonstrate strong and unified beliefs on how to achieve success?
- Do they demonstrate a positive attitude towards change, regardless of whether they agree with it or not?
- Do they effectively support one another through change?
- Do they challenge one another's thinking?
- Do they regularly ask questions?
- Do they speak up and share honest opinions?
- Do they welcome input and ideas from one another?
- Do they learn from one another, especially learning from mistakes?
- Do they encourage risk-taking and innovative thinking?
- Do they demonstrate commitment and continuous improvement?
- Do they dedicate time to improving how the team works together to achieve goals?
- Do they demonstrate accountability for the team's vision and results?

The table on the next page is a representation that shows the differences between a fixed mindset and a growth mindset in an individual.

CULTURE – VALUES AND HABITS

Fixed Mindset	Growth Mindset
It's too complicated; I can't	Hmm, I can. Let me try.
Thinks personal failure defines them.	Sees failure as a learning process.
Avoids challenges to avoid failures	Embrace challenges.
Quits easily	Learns from feedback.
Feels threatened by others' success	Feels inspired by others' success
Thinks intelligence and talent are fixed	Believes intelligence and talent can be developed.
It feels the effort is fruitless.	Believes effort is the path to mastery.
I don't have any good ideas.	Let me think about it and get back to you.
I don't know what to do.	How about we try this?
Feedback is criticism and a sign of failure.	Feedback is an opportunity to grow and improve.
Afraid to admit when they don't know something	Willing to say, "I don't know" - and eager to learn.
I never did it, I don't know how to do it.	I never did it, but I will learn and do it.
I failed at it	I learned from it

TEAMWORK

"If you want to go quickly, go alone. If you want to go far, go together."
- African proverb

Any avenue that requires a group of people to achieve a common goal entails teamwork, which is a collaborative effort of each individual to achieve an expected result. Collaboration introduces harmony into the workplace; it promotes unity and support between co-workers by exchanging knowledge and ideas. Team members share their creativity in brainstorming towards the achievement of a set goal or in solving problems.

An essential factor to note is making a diverse team a winning team as well. The culture of winning must be ingrained in the group. When a team can work together, it can solve daunting challenges with relative ease because there is mutual support and trust from its members. Therefore, it is a win-win situation for both the team and the manager, making a manager effective. The absence of teamwork dramatically affects productivity and generally creates a very haphazard atmosphere. Companies with more excellent collaboration always have a competitive advantage and reach their objectives faster because tasks are assigned according to team members' strengths and expertise to enhance efficiency.

I once participated in a management training where I was attached to a group of ten to take on a project which would give us a better understanding of the theoretical aspect of our study. As opposed to having a much larger learning group, with the risk of limited opportunity to speak or make contributions, this project required a smaller group to encourage self-expression with people I was not well acquainted with before being grouped. Still, we had to come together to complete the assignment and make a group presentation based on our findings.

However, a particular group member always seemed to have a different opinion about how the rest of us handled the task and insisted we do things his way. He also made sure to let the team know about his foreign educational background, which made him feel superior to the rest of us. He instinctively assumed a leadership role without being elected and wanted to be in charge of the situation. Constant disagreements ensued, which prompted a member of the group to opt-out of the project because she was uncomfortable with the status of things. The few of us who remained motivated carried out the research and survey, then put together some data.

As we approached the presentation day, the egotistical fellow seemed to have finally settled with our ideas and offered to be the group's speaker. We were glad to have no more antagonism come from him and happily gave him a hard copy of our data so he could study in preparation for the presentation. Eventually, the D-day came, and to our most tremendous shock, what he presented was utterly different from what we had jointly worked on for the past two weeks. We were stunned but powerless to interrupt a presentation that had already begun for fear of how it may have reflected on the team.

After the 15-minute presentation, the instructor questioned him about the processes that led to producing the data, but he stood there petrified, unable to speak clearly. The instructor then called on the rest of us to list our contributions towards the research on the findings. We explained how what was supposed to be a team effort was hijacked by one individual who did not want to cooperate. Our presentation became invalid, and as a result, we failed the exercise. The instructor explained that the exercise's primary purpose was not in the works. It was merely to demonstrate the efficacy of teamwork and collaboration and measure how much of it we portrayed, which we did not display. He also mentioned something that resonated with me: to manage a team of people and foster a group mindset, you must demonstrate it first. Thus, as a leader, you must be a team player and not a commander.

The example shows how a lack of teamwork and collaboration can derail the goals of a group. The team will undoubtedly stray away from the vision, and this will affect the results. Every member of a team possesses unique thoughts and approach to any task, and this is crucial in solving a problem or reaching a goal.

Team members must be able to freely and reasonably express their points of view without causing conflict. In directing my team, I gauge their emotional levels and identify their individual qualities to help them apply themselves properly and give feedback that does not discourage their efforts and kill their morale.

HOW TO ENCOURAGE TEAMWORK

Team size

When it comes to team size, small is good. In building a team, you must understand that a team's size must be proportional to its goals, as this will reflect in its performances. As a leader, you must be strategic when setting up your team; you must have an adequate number of people that can support and carry out the objectives efficiently. Most high-performing teams I led had been single digit. In my personal experience, as team size increases, people increasingly underestimate the resources required to complete the projects.

Individualism

Each team member has a unique ability and perception that could be of great use; bringing different individuals together facilitates a supply of other ideas and various approaches to solving a problem and achieving an objective.

Morale

The level at which individuals in a team feel motivated will most certainly reflect the quality of work they produce. Therefore, you must be a 'cheer-leader' who spurs your squad on and encourages them when they feel overwhelmed by the project's expectations.

Codependency

If it takes one person two days to get a task done, splitting the same job between ten people will have it finished in under an hour. Members of a team should rely on each other and be accountable to one another to achieve success.

Where there is codependency, team members can motivate one another because their activities are closely linked. As such, productivity requires a joint effort, which boosts support and better communication within a team.

Competition

Healthy competition within teams keeps them on their toes. A way to do this is creating an incentive for better performance; recognizing the best performers on their achievements could significantly improve the synergy of your team and boost excellence.

Hierarchy

Sometimes, teams are made up of people with different levels of skill, knowledge, and position. It could sometimes inform their behavior towards one another and might encourage loafing.

Some members instinctively leave the bulk of the work for other team members they feel are their subordinate to pick up the slack; this could affect a team's dynamic and cause poor communication.

Communication

One of the critical things that highlight the efficacy of teamwork is the ability to think collectively and agree on an idea to be carried out; this is impossible without proper communication.

Good communication amongst team members ensures that everyone receives the same message.

Feedback should be encouraged to have every member who has been brought up to speed be at the same level of information; where there is effective communication, there is less conflict and antagonism.

Bonding

Team bonding is a point at which team members agree. Besides merely knowing how to work with one another, good relationships within a team are vital to enhancing its effectiveness.

Members of a team should be tightly-knit; there is always a great deal of trust in well-bonded units. To achieve projected goals, individuals in a group must reach a point where they understand each other's strengths and weaknesses and support one another when needed.

Before we build a house, we must lay out the foundation. In the same way, team bonding is one of the critical ingredients for a stronger foundation in a team. Having good relationships and bonding means all perspectives are well heard.

WINNING AS A TEAM

"Managers should build themselves to do anything, but not everything. Delegation is the key to scale."

— **Sharad Bajaj**

As a team-lead, the responsibility to take your team from where you began to the level you envisioned rests upon your shoulders, as you have to navigate your ship in the direction you want it to go.

You need to understand that you cannot do it alone, and as such, the success of a team is not yours alone but is shared among all team members. To build a winning team, you must know when to direct your team and when to stay in the background and allow the team to function independently.

Therefore, you must strive for stability. One of the indicators of synergy in a group is its ability to perform smoothly even in your absence because they have a framework that guides them.

To build a winning team, you must know where your team stands based on every member's abilities and try to spot the weakest link, then help bring them to a stable position. Strengthening the most vulnerable connection involves constant encouragement.

Winning as a team requires partnership and a strong culture for every individual to align with the vision. There is less focus on individual differences in a winning team as all eyes must be on the goal and conform to the team culture. A winning team is like a family; members are more expressive about their opinions and challenges and are not afraid to ask one another for help and guidance.

There is also a great deal of mentorship involved as it is clear that individuals nurture one another in such teams, which builds togetherness.

As a manager, I always endeavor to involve my group in team-building exercises to harness togetherness and team spirit. I still want people to win together and work together. There was a time my team and I were involved in a team-building exercise. In this game, everyone was given a balloon and a pin, and people were supposed to take out their balloons without popping them.

However, something strange began to happen; some individuals started popping other people's balloons so that their balloons would be safe. Whereas, it could have been easier for everyone to protect their balloons so that nobody's balloon is popped, and everyone wins together. This was an important discovery in discerning teamwork and togetherness in a group.

Another exercise was also undertaken, where the team was divided into two parts and given random names. Both teams had a box of randomly placed letters and needed to compile a list that best fits their group names.

Whoever compiled the best list would win the game. I noticed that when a team picked a letter that doesn't include their name but is closer to the other team's name, they handed the letter over to the other team.

In this way, they understood that although it was a competition, both teams needed to work together to get faster results. As a manager, it is vital to infuse the culture of winning as a team within your group. These steps will guide you to build a winning team:

Create an action plan

An objective is more likely to be actualized when it is in a written form. Every structured organization uses an action plan to carry out every project to conduct operations. There is a high level of specificity to every activity carried out by a team.

The first step to take before deploying team members to carry out their respective roles is to have a well-developed plan, a laid-down guide on what to do, when to do it, and whom to assign given roles. It creates a framework of expectation for each individual in your team, and such expectations must be realistic.

Enhance their understanding

While it is impressive to watch your team take the initiative in handling tasks, it is also important to arm them with the necessary information they need to excel. You must be transparent in laying out your expectations of them, allow them to ask questions to gain clarity, and explain the mapped-out plan as best you can. Do a demonstration if needed as long as it helps you play your part in preventing confusion from arising.

Establish a common ground

Recognizing the things that differentiate members of your team is essential to strike a balance. If you have a diverse group, you need to introduce a strong culture that every member can identify with; you must go out of your way to make every member feels included, especially those that seem like the oddballs in the group.

This enables them to come out of their shell and give their best to realizing the unified goal.

Every member of a team must be comfortable enough to share their views. Every team briefing should have a time set out for members to throw in their ideas and contribute their thoughts to foster team growth, and there must be a good spotlight on all team members to encourage them to be more active.

Curb favoritism

Often, leaders pick a favorite, someone they are more comfortable and more inclined to assign specific tasks to or even exempt from certain team activities that every member should usually be involved in. As a leader, you must be wary of this as it might adversely affect your team when you keep the spotlight on a single team member. It often discourages team members as they quickly feel like outsiders and unappreciated. Therefore, to manage a team effectively, you must show equal value to every member to keep them engaged and maintain morale.

Work with your team

To manage a winning team, you must practice participative leadership. You must indulge in teamwork. In participating, you must also take care not to disrupt the progress through micro-management.

This could significantly affect their confidence and ability to perform optimally, give them a sense that you have faith in their skill by taking a step back to let them work. The essence of participating is solely to offer guidance where needed; hence you must make this clear to your team.

It is essential to check with your team without micromanaging regularly. You can do this in different ways; One way is through an initial team survey that generates data on how members perceive team interactions and functioning. A survey can include topics such as commitment, trust, communication, and conflict resolution. You can organize the study at least quarterly to determine the progress and effectiveness of the processes.

Another way to check a team's "pulse" is to have regular open discussions about what is working and what is not. Practice every day informal conversations that keep communication channels open. Once you notice the ineffectiveness of a process, the most crucial part is to fix it as soon as possible so that the team remains encouraged to provide feedback.

CHAPTER SUMMARY

- As a leader and a manager, it is essential to build a winning as a team culture in your team to attain meaningful success.
- Culture eats strategy for breakfast. The foundation of every successful group is a well-defined culture. Excellent strategy without a solid culture will eventually fall short of expectations.
- A winning culture serves as a guide for a team to achieve its goals.
- Certain elements form the foundation of a right culture. They are
  1. Diversity, Inclusion, and Belonging (DIB)
  2. Winning as a team
  3. Teamwork
  4. Growth mindset
  5. Psychological safety

  These elements, when effectively combined, build a solid culture.
- As a manager, you must learn to be adaptable primarily due to the coronavirus pandemic.
- You must learn how to motivate and keep your team productive while they all work remotely.
- You must be innovative and abreast with the changes in technology to aid your work.

REFLECTIONS

What will an ideal team culture look like to you? Can you list five core values and habits you want your team to live by?

Reflect:
_____
_____
_____
_____

How do you ensure everyone in your team live by the culture of the company?

Reflect:
_____
_____
_____
_____

Does your team feel comfortable owning up to mistakes or place blame on others when mistakes are made?

Reflect:
_____
_____
_____
_____

Does your team avoid difficult conversations that can make you or team members uncomfortable?

CULTURE – VALUES AND HABITS

Reflect:
_____
_____
_____
_____

What is your role in your organization to incorporate diversity, inclusion, and belonging?

Reflect:
_____
_____
_____
_____

What makes a team function successfully?

Reflect:
_____
_____
_____
_____

What strategies would you use to motivate your team?

Reflect:
_____
_____
_____
_____

CHAPTER 6

WHITE SPACE

"A great leader is dispensable when it comes to their tasks and actions. And indispensable when it comes to their thought and vision."

-Ankur Warikoo

As a manager, you need to remember you are the team leader. A lot is expected of you. Not being at your best is not an option you should willingly consider. It is one you should intentionally avoid.

"Trust that white space - pause is essential. It allows reflecting on the situation in real-time while the context is fresh."

- Sharad Bajaj

    White space is undoubtedly a metaphor for pausing. Different people use it in various ways in capturing opportunities and connecting the dots. It's like taking a few stops and exploring while on an eight-hour drive - it will make your journey more meaningful.

    Many people tend to hold onto the idea of overworking themselves and pushing themselves beyond their physical and mental limits as a sign of success that is worthy of respect. They ignore the overtly glaring importance of "white space."

    Some time ago, I realized I was mostly drowning in meetings, emails, status reports, fire drills, and similar duties. I became acculturated to tolerating the things that were really exhausting my capacity to be productive. I was out of energy but needed to focus on why I couldn't connect the dots. I had to intentionally stop the madness and create some time in my schedule. I called that time white space. It is a time for strategy, creativity, introspection, digging deep, and looking at the bigger picture. It is time for mental exploration. I initially did not do all of these because I was too busy. So, I started creating blocks of time in my calendar time for thinking. While driving to work, during morning walks, and in between meetings, I make out time for Myself.

White space is not just any time; it is a strategic "pause" between activities. It is time for you and your personal growth. It is the time when an individual rediscovers themselves, connects the dots in a fast-paced work environment. White space is a crucial topic because many people are doing an excellent job of ignoring it.

As a manager, I cannot overemphasize the importance of white space. It is a space everyone should have for themselves. I describe the white space as a period of reflection and observation. You assess your thoughts and break them down into bits to understand them better.

It also includes the reconciliation of ideas and events in past meetings. I always make sure to wrap my sessions five minutes earlier than the agreed finishing time. The whole textbook for an average manager is filled with meetings and deadlines.

Managers must participate in these meetings, and the deadlines met. So, the one place you can find time for self-reflection and reconciliation of your thoughts is the space in between, referred to as the white space.

I utilize the five minutes left after meetings for reflections. I sit back to process and ruminate on decisions agreed upon and take the next course of action.

You need white space to put things in perspective. The white space helps you think critically, and critical thinking gives birth to productive business decisions. Often, we tend not to value white space's power, only to discover that we are experiencing difficulties connecting the dots. So, we may end up moving from meeting to meeting like a ghost; no bearings, no focused movement.

As a manager, you will face many responsibilities with little or no time to think. Every manager needs white space. It is, in fact, a mandatory requirement. The white space provides us with a time for reflection, a time to decompress and access our high cognitive function. It continuously builds your capacity to lead more effectively.

In times of increasing demands, uncertainties, complexities, and ambiguity, we are willing to address our strengths and challenges and work together to produce a positive outcome. Most people prefer it to be a simple check and balance. It checks your actions and balances your decisions or options. Without this, you are stuck in a deep ocean taking in more and more water as you are drowning.

Sometime late last year, I caught myself drowning. It was getting to the Christmas holidays, and the office was rounding up for the year. Many meetings were held, deadlines were increasing, and so many things were happening at once. I was moving around on a very tight, busy schedule. I barely even had the time to eat during the working days. The work was overwhelming and stressful, and I completely ignored a time for white space. I kept moving from meeting to meeting until I broke down one day.

On that fateful day, the discussions went on as usual. A team member threw a direct question at me. I ended up narrating something entirely out of line with what was going on at the moment. It was so out of line that my team members all busted out into uncontrollable laughter. I couldn't help but join them. There and then, I decided we all needed to take a break.

The meeting degenerated into one of small talks and laughter. Everyone became relaxed, and it led to a better productive time in the next meeting. I learned a precious lesson that day. It taught me not to ignore some me-time. No matter how busy I get, it is essential to infuse it in.

We learn to tire and wear out. The human body and mind are not made for constant work and thinking, and it is built for rest too; this is why we sleep at night or observe a moment of rest or siesta during the day. Without creating white space, you are left in a constant battle and pursuit of challenges and not taking absolute control of it. If I had continued without creating white space, I would have ended up with a terrible situation on my hands. It would have resulted in unproductivity.

"People who have had little self-reflection live life in a huge reality blind spot."

- Bryant McGill

This powerful quote from American international bestselling author Bryant carefully illustrates the power of self-reflection and "white space." The topic of " white space" is not practiced enough in the corporate sector.

The crucial question many ask is, "can I create that white space in my busy schedule?" and my answer remains an absolute yes! Yes, you can, and yes, you should. It is essential and needs to be fulfilled and given time. You can create periods for this in your calendar. I refer to this period created as blocks (time blocks). I fight personal battles every day, and as a manager, I have come to the point of realization that in my day-to-day activities, I create blocks stipulated at different moments of the day.

I make at least thirty minutes block each day for my white space. I have blocked from eight to nine, twelve to two-thirty, and five to five-thirty. These blocks are solely reserved for me and just me alone.

I am left to think about concluded meetings, meetings, and many more, except in emergency cases requiring immediate attention. My white space ritual is carried out daily, and I make sure never to miss it. The improvement I have made over the years is evident, and its positive contribution to my work can also not be ignored.

Think of the white space as a slow-motion video. When watching a video, you are left with a screen and images; these images tell you a story. In a swift motion, the message behind the video might not be understood. On the other hand, a slow-motion video offers you more options. You are left to view the images at a slower pace, and as such, you can pick up little details. These details in slow motion are what your white space is to you. It is that slow-motion video where you can relax and view everything in a broader picture. You are in a state of observation that allows you to connect the dots, sort out issues, and increase competence.

You might often need to push hard in adjusting your schedule to create a time for white space. You can also give the white space a name that helps create some urgency to the time. It can be named strategic thinking, connecting the dots, white space, relaxation time, or whatever term suits your personality.

I called my white space "connecting the dots." You are left with more time, and it becomes a daily reminder that pushes you into strategic thinking.

Before the pandemic outbreak, I could go through meetings for two days or more without having time to rest, sit back, and think. When I observed these happenings, I ensured to adopt the white space strategy.

I had to consciously remind myself about what or what not to do, rethink situations, and re-strategize. I also made sure to teach my team members the importance of white space. And it was amazing to watch their progress after we created time to reflect. I also have moments where my team and I drink tea or coffee and casually chat. The famous saying of "all work and no play makes Jack a dull boy" can fully be understood in this context.

Despite the pandemic changing the natural order of things such as the daily routine of going to work, going to recreational places, restaurants, and many others, the work situation has remained the same. The only difference is the work from home policy that most organizations have implemented. Home is simply an easy virtual process where people can carry out their tasks and attend virtual meetings. This change in working patterns has changed the need for people to be physically present. Consequently, many people have complained about being overworked, which may be accurate as meetings can sometimes stretch till late in the night.

The idea of comfort while working from your home has somewhat beclouded the need for rest. Many individuals stay on their couch or bed for many hours stuck in a meeting.

WHITE SPACE

Of course, such a pattern is terrible as people, including me, have forgotten to pay attention to our white spaces.

I observed that I wasn't adhering to my white space-time religiously anymore. I had to change the narrative of my remote work patterns. Presently, I try to get a minimum of two hours of break each day. For my holiday, I make sure to eat healthily, relax, strategically think, develop new ideas, or do something as mundane as catching up with a favorite television show. Your white space must not necessarily center on "strategic thinking" alone. It could be a fun simple relaxing activity like playing a game on your phone.

The white space is your "you space." Use it as it deems fit. So long as it is benefiting you mentally and sometimes physically. The white space created, of course, increased my team's overall general performance. Working under stress and pressure is never the best. When I feel stressed, I close my eyes, breathe for a minute, and observe during my breaks. It is a powerful meditative exercise that helps me relax during the day.

Another thing to remember is that you can use white space daily, weekly, monthly, or yearly. Taking a vacation is a white space. In some organizations, team members are entitled to leave twice a year. Taking that vacation is akin to taking "me time." You do not have to travel far away for your holiday; just relaxing and taking time off work to refresh your brain and mind is sufficient.

Also, weekly "me time" can be moments where you access activities done for a week. You make sure to cross your I's and dot your T's. The differences lay in the time frames. I still, however, insist that every manager should create time daily for self-reflection. Creating a white space is vital for your mental and physical performance.

It would be best if you always remembered that you are human and not a robot. Humans need rest; even robots do. For extra busy persons, you must prioritize. There should be a constant daily reminder of its importance. White space allows your team to build skill sets that improve both balance and performance. You need to push this as part of your team culture. You can make out 2-3 days every three months outside the day-to-day job for innovative sessions.

As stated above, the importance of white space can never be overemphasized. However, if you feel it is, I would like you to remember that white space continually pushes you to control situations better.

It helps you to move from the passenger's seat to the driver's seat. Of course, there would be times when you may be pushed back to the passenger's seat again because of so many responsibilities that might burden you. But the white space is always there to drive you right back up. It is a journey. You must fight hard to strive and win. "Keep moving; you are not meant to be stuck. God gave you feet, not roots."

HOW TO CREATE WHITE SPACE

- You can carry out these in five easy steps.
- Plan a schedule on your calendar
- Go for a 5-10-minute walk after lunch.
- Make sure to follow and use the time allocated.
- It's okay to sit in silence.
- Request not to be disturbed
- Connecting the dots, reconciliation, and critical strategizing is okay.
- One-minute breathing, close your eyes, observe.

CHAPTER SUMMARY

The white space helps you think critically, and critical thinking gives birth to productive business decisions. White space is a strategic pause. White space is a short period helps you to reflect and observe. You assess your thoughts and break them down into bits to understand them better. White space provides us with a time for reflection, a time to decompress and access our high cognitive function. White space continuously builds your capacity to lead more effectively.

REFLECTIONS

As a manager, are you able to take breaks between meetings?
Reflect:

___

Do you have blocks of time in your calendar where you think and respond?
Reflect:

___

Are you able to think clearly and appropriately before responding?
Reflect:

___

Do you have time for lunch breaks?
Reflect:

CHAPTER 7

THERE IS NO MAP

"Stay committed to your decisions, but stay flexible in your approach."

– **Tony Robbins**

Due to the surge in information consumption, the modern-day and age has equipped many individuals with various tools with a nondiscriminatory amount of free access. Innovation is driving the world's changes, and the first people to fail will be map-followers, non-risk takers, and conformists. These kinds of people will get lost in the fast-paced world we live in today. It is unfortunate because they were told to "follow the system," and it has failed them over time.

People can now get any information they need at their fingertips. The advent of the internet and social media has made information on any subject pretty accessible. News now comes in varied formats; in hard copies and e-formats. Most authors these days publish paperback and e-book versions of their books. Not only are materials diverse in numbers, but you can get them in whatever format you desire.

Consequently, there is more circulation of information, easy access to this information, and a certain co-dependency on the published information. Many people assume reading and following a rigorous step-by-step process gets them to whatever goal they hope to achieve at the end of the day. For the most part, it is a false assumption, as most people tend to box themselves in and end up working with processes that do not equip them to become their best selves.

There is no doubt that information overload is prevalent nowadays. There is a wide range of information that provides tips and guidance on any topic that interests you. There is also a wide range of audiences consuming this information. However, some people who share this information pass it on as absolutes, giving this information as facts instead of opinions. Therefore, many individuals may wonder why certain information, when applied, doesn't work out for them. Instead, they are sometimes left worse than when they started.

However, you must note that seeking information or guides on becoming a manager is an excellent step to take. But you must remember that not all words are useful. Most information given is merely opinions of the said author who wishes to share their knowledge to equip you better. There is no set guidance or silver bullets to becoming the best manager. There is no monopoly on this information that puts you on the path of greatness.

The information you need and want is varied based on your demand and the type of organization or work you carry out, and your management style. It also centers on what kind of information you need. You can sieve through information when received.

One of the qualities of a good leader is how well information received is handled and implemented. When dealing with information that directly affects how you carry out your daily activities, it is crucial to seek out information that would not cause a case of rigidity in your professional and personal life. It is also okay to fail and try again. The path to success is full of challenges and lessons. Don't stop if something does not work. I firmly believe leaders are good readers. Read a lot, and apply your knowledge.

"Remember the two benefits of failure. First, if you do fail, you learn what doesn't work; and second, the failure allows you to try a new approach."

- Roger Von Oech

What is a map? A map is a visual or laid down guidance that guides and leads you to your destination choice. It is an essential tool for getting to your destination. Most of us use Google Maps to discover new places like restaurants, religious houses, gyms, and much more. However, it may be rigid. It shows you only one destination point to another point. You are left to follow a step-by-step process to lead you to your destination point. Now the vital question; is there only one path to be followed when getting to the end of the destination?

Your answer is as good as mine; there is no single pathway in getting to your chosen destination. That is why roads are made in multiples and intersect. In this way, you have options and many ways to get to your point of destination.

Imagine if we only had one route to get to our destination points? I would imagine a chaotic mass of human traffic, as everyone would be scrambling to get ahead. Nobody would arrive then. The map analogy typifies every endeavor of life. Why think there is a map to becoming a manager and assume the road is a straight, narrow, and rigid system that requires you to follow X, Y, Z to achieve your goals?

These questions and many more are questions you need to ask yourself when dealing with a situation where you see yourself assuming a map leads you to your answers generally in life.

I also used to think there was just one way to get the desired result. However, there is a lot I have learned in my professional career as a manager. During my early management days, I desperately sought new ways to improve myself. I went as far as purchasing self-help books that would assist me in achieving my goals. I listened to audio teachings in my spare time too. I hoped to be the best but went about it in a relatively ineffective way, as I was slowly turning into a rigid, stiff version of myself.

I rejected change as much as possible, and I always insisted on a specific pattern and way to do things, causing a strained relationship between my team members and me. I assumed I was doing the right things according to the information I consumed and followed each process's instructions accordingly. If my book said, "yelling was the best way to command your audience," I would walk into the office the next day and yell my guts out.

I kept following this negative pattern until I realized I was following a map that led nowhere but a dangerous place. I was lucky enough to make this realization early enough. My negative outbursts hadn't gotten to the point where they became habits. That would have been detrimental to not just my professional career but my personal life as well. I started putting everything into perspective. If something works for X person, it may not necessarily work for me. Generalization is the enemy of innovation. Let's not put everyone in the same boat.

Modern managers should be flexible and adaptable. Adaptability is an essential trait a manager must have to ensure longevity in the corporate world. Adaptability is one trait that has seen the human race and other animals survive over changing times. Species that were not able to adapt ultimately became extinct. This is also true of managers, and you must be flexible and adaptable to the changes in management styles to remain in the game. While adaptability is something, we can all benefit from, it's particularly critical for leaders. As a leader leaps from being a supervisor to a middle manager, and finally, to a senior position, they will need to adapt to management style changes.

Leadership roles become more complex as you progress in an organization - requiring more subtle influencing and persuading skills. Also, the higher a leader's position, the greater the need to learn how to empower, delegate, form strategic alliances, and let go of skills that worked earlier for them but are no longer useful.

"Learning to collaborate is a part of equipping yourself for effectiveness, problem-solving, innovation and life-long learning in an ever-changing networked economy."

- Don Tapscott

Another thing to learn as a manager is the art of flexibility. It would help if you remembered that you are flexible and need to adapt and embrace the challenges quickly. Things and times are changing, work patterns are also changing, and the industry is evolving. Similarly, the educational system and many other things are adjusting to the current times. So, the need for flexibility is imperative to keeping up with the pace and delivering the right job with the changing times.

In 2020, many managers have learned how to work remotely, keep their team motivated, handle performance management, and create a successful work situation amidst the pandemic. Thus, the need for flexibility and adaptability as a manager. The pandemic has moved people from the physical working spaces to virtual ones. Managers have learned to manage meetings via video calls, which has somewhat improved their computer skills. Managers have also known how to get tasks done despite not having the team physically together, highlighting the power of adaptability. The need to push and bend you to take new paths you wouldn't have ordinarily taken makes it such a powerful tool for every manager to possess. Since your roles are evolving, you need to adapt to situations and new approaches to tackle different problems, as this is vital for your professional growth as a manager.

Change is a constant thing in life, and so, as a manager, you must be willing to embrace change whenever it happens. The world itself constantly evolves; we've moved from the Stone Age to the Analog Age, and now to the Digital Age. Changes will always occur. The past ten years have ushered in a wave of technological advancements that have further propelled the world and made our lives much more comfortable. You must ensure that change is positive, helpful, and pushes you to attain high levels for yourself. So, embrace that change today.

Embracing changes may mean dealing with anxiety, uncertainty, and fear, you should expect these, and you mustn't see them as absurd. Early in my managerial journey, I encountered many challenges in a bid to become a better manager. Most of these challenges were self-inflicted, and I was on my way to self-sabotaging.

I had irrational fear and anxiety. Many questions ran through my mind, one of which was if people would accept the new me. But one emotion I finally felt after going through all these emotions was happiness. I felt much joy after observing the growth achieved with my new found changes. I was a better team leader, my team members' performances were off the charts, and my social interactions were good. It was such a great emotion to experience.

Another beautiful emotion I experienced after making my changes would be freedom—following a map that led me nowhere. I learned management in its proper form. The ability to manage wasn't going to come from a book; it was going to come from me. I am management, and management is me. It would help if you always remembered this.

"The conventional definition of management is getting work done through people, but real management is developing people through work."

- Agha Hasan Abedi

It is the manager's job to implement a culture of adaptability in their team so that when changes are needed, the team can adjust quickly and seamlessly. Change is inevitable, and when it does come, the manager should keep this in mind, be ready for it, and welcome it with open arms.

Becoming a good manager is being ready to take risks and accepting responsibilities. As a manager, you are a risk-taker. You are the team leader, and as a team leader, your job is being ready to make difficult choices that may or may not involve work out on a project. Your ability to be a critical thinker prepares you for risk-taking.

You should have it at the back of your mind that things may not always go as planned, and when that happens, you must be able to proffer other options because there's still a chance that plans may not work. Therefore, you consider that. As a manager, team members look up to you and expect you to make the best decisions. Becoming a manager is accepting that you are not just a leader, but you are a risk-taker. You take the fall for the team and celebrate the team's successes together. Therefore, you must note that leadership is servitude, nothing more or less.

Becoming a manager goes way beyond theoretical explanations. You have to strive to become a better version of yourself. Effective leadership then is determined by the results you provide rather than the attributes you portray. So, become the manager you want to see today!

CHAPTER SUMMARY

There is no map in assuming responsibility and becoming a leader. As a manager, you will face many challenges and obstacles; persistence is the key to success. As a leader, you must learn to forge your path while learning from the experiences of others. Always strive to be innovative and flexible in all you do. Don't be afraid of taking risks.

REFLECTIONS

As a manager, do you consider yourself innovative, and how has this impacted your team?
Reflect:
___

When was the last time you took risks, and what was the outcome?
Reflect:
___

Do you encourage flexibility in your team, and what steps do you take to ensure your remote team is flexible and productive?
Reflect:
___

What's one thing you can do to improve your team's performance?
Reflect:
___

CHAPTER 8

THE ULTIMATE CHOICE

"You gain strength, courage, and confidence by every experience in which you stop to look fear in the face. You must do the thing you think you cannot do."

- Eleanor Roosevelt

Choosing to become a manager is a conscious, deliberate effort only you can make. Like all choices, it needs to be mulled over, broken down into parts, weighed, and finally decided upon, then actions as the next decision line.

Being a manager is much more than the title, and it goes beyond the power gain you perceived to have at the end of the day. Of course, it may come with financial gains, don't get me wrong, but using that as the primary motivation to make your choice in becoming a manager is only a recipe for disaster.

You might have been thinking about this for a long time now, anticipating being the boss, assuming responsibilities, and tackling more challenging projects that require those expert skills you have worked for and gained over the years.

You are ready for it now, and you think it's the right time to go for the job as a manager. However, are you genuinely prepared and making the right choice? Is this job for you? Are you going into it for the right reasons? Many such questions you need to ask yourself before embarking on the journey to becoming a manager.

A little story of mine I would love to share. Earlier in the book, I stated how my journey to being a manager started. I was born and raised in India. You might call me a big dreamer, as I had big dreams I wanted to fulfill and achieve. Failure was never an option for me, and I carried that thought along with me. It comes as no surprise that my dreams led me from one continent to another. Whenever I look back, I remember my young self, who believed in the older self I am today. I knew I wanted to become a manager, and I went for it regardless of the obstacles I faced.

It is never easy. Life throws obstacles at us, and we must be ready to scale these hurdles, however. The goal is to get to our final destination.

Now the first step in choosing to become a manager requires you to have some clarity about why you want to become a manager and have a passion for it. Nothing morphs out of the blue. What I have learned so far, if you really wanted to achieve something in life, have an exclusive interest in it, and pursue it passionately.

Do you want to become a manager? What are your plans? What is that driving force that pushes you in wanting to make this career choice for yourself? Do you see yourself doing this? You can't rely on others' suggestions or affirmations that "Yes" to that question is the right answer. You have to dig deeper.

In my experience, many people learn this the hard way. I remember there was a rock star best performing engineer in one of my teams who'd expressed a strong desire to become a manager.

A year into the role, this person was miserable. He realized he didn't like his day-to-day tasks as a manager, and he wasn't very good at it. Later he happily went back to being a senior-level individual contributor.

I had the opportunity to talk to this engineer to learn about his experience as a manager. In his own words, "I first had a tough time as a manager because I quickly and painfully realized that the skills that got me noticed in the team and moved me up to managerial role were not the same that would get the job done or help me keep moving. Being a rock star engineer and being a rock star manager required two totally different sets of skills. Both are important for any successful team.

Let me clarify that the struggles new managers face represents the norm, not the exception. These aren't less capable managers operating in dysfunctional organizations.

They're ordinary people facing everyday adjustment problems. Most of them survive the transition and learn to function in their new role. But imagine how much more effective they would be if the change were less traumatic.

Becoming a manager is not achieved in a day and required unlearning a mindset and habits that had initially made me highly successful during my early career days—and relearning new professional habits as a new identity emerges.

The new manager internalizes new ways of thinking and being and discovers new ways of measuring success and deriving work satisfaction. Not surprisingly, this kind of change is tasking. As one new manager notes, "I never knew a promotion could be so painful."

New managers inevitably ponder on two questions: "Will I like my new role as manager?" and "Will I be good at managing the team and projects?" Of course, there are no immediate answers; they come only with experience. And these two questions are often accompanied by an even more unsettling one: "Who am I becoming?"

Based on my experience, the transition is often harder than it needs to be because of new managers' misconceptions about their new roles. Their ideas about what it means to be a manager hold some truth. But, because these notions are simplistic and incomplete, they create false expectations that individuals struggle to reconcile with the reality of the manager's life. By acknowledging the following misconceptions—some of which are just plain myths, and accepting reality, new managers have a far greater chance of success.

The right choices are rooted in knowing that becoming a manager is for knowledge and serving people in your team and customers. It is to learn new skills, your team's growth, and bring the best out of your team members and yourself. It is also knowing that you would need to work with others.

Working with others includes learning and understanding the art of proper and effective communication, being tolerant, and willing to help and coach. Making that right choice is knowing that you are no longer an individual contributor, and your decisions will have to be in the best interest of your team and the business, not you. You are now part of a team, and the entire team looks up to you.

The last step is loving your job. This love drives you to earn the position you hope to attain. Not loving your job affects everyone.

As a manager, you are a reflection of your team. Never forget that. If your actions show a disinterest on your path, it should come as no surprise when the team also shows signs of weariness and complete disregard for their job and performance. Your visions and goals need to align with the right choice and reason(s).

Develop yourself, your skills, and gain more experience. Choosing to be a manager is knowing that it won't happen in a day, but with time, effort, and hard work, success is inevitable. Managers listen more - you must ask yourself if you are ready to listen more and talk less.

Before I became a manager, I was holding other individual contributor positions. I knew my end goal, but it never stopped me from shining in the particular work I was involved in. I made sure to put in my best, develop a new set of skills, learn and unlearn, and gather as much experience as I could muster.

A good manager knows that starting small is not doing badly. I was not fortunate enough to have a college degree to become a manager. I went through several levels to arrive at my current position. It was not easy, but I knew it was achievable. Look at numerical figures.

They have a strict pattern that they follow; you don't jump from the number one to twenty; it never works out. You start small, at level one, followed by levels two and three, until you reach the "boss level".

That is how this works. It is small, comfortable, steady steps that take you to your final destination. Of course, you can make enormous strides, but the rule at the end of the day is you are climbing from one stage to the other. It is like climbing a staircase. Some decide to walk, some run, and some jog. The whole point is that you take those steps at the end of the day. So be ready for action.

Making that choice has the realization that you would be a leader. Now being a leader isn't becoming an authoritarian. It is becoming a person who leads the way while taking into consideration the feelings of everyone. Yes, you heard right, you must include everyone.

That is why you are a leader. No member of your team is allowed to feel marginalized or not heard. They should all be heard, allowed to contribute, and their contributions included. Being a leader is also knowing that all the praise does not go to you alone. It is for the team. I always make sure that my team knows that we are all to take glory in moments of celebration. We are one.

In this sense, management is like any other job: There are upsides and downsides, specific skills, biases, and mindsets. And as a result, not everyone should feel compelled to aspire to become a manager.

For example, if you don't love cooking, you shouldn't be a chef. If you're not into buildings, you shouldn't be an architect. And if you're not excited about specific things managers do, you likely shouldn't want to become a manager.

Most times, when asked to explain their role, new managers tend to focus on the rights and privileges that come with being the manager; they assume the position will give them more authority, freedom, and autonomy to do what they think is best for the organization. No longer, in the words of one, will they be "burdened by the unreasonable demands of team members."

Being a leader is much more than you may expect it to be. It is not dressing up and barking commands, as you see in the movies. It is learning to tolerate, communicate, and work collectively as a team. Furthermore, it is accepting that others have a say. You are not the only one in the room. Most importantly, you are not the smartest in the room; your team's collective effort is better than individual effort.

THE ULTIMATE CHOICE

> "The challenge of leadership is to be strong, but not be rude; be kind, but not weak; be bold, but not bully; be thoughtful, but not lazy; be humble, but not timid; be proud, but not arrogant; have humor, but without folly."
>
> **- Jim Rohn**

Since I started the leadership journey, I have always kept a positive outlook on people and situations, and I recommend that you do the same as well. Whatever anyone says or does, always assume a positive outlook. You will be amazed at how your approach to a person or a situation changes when you examine them differently. When you accept a negative view, you quickly become angry. On the flip side, a positive outlook brings amazement.

You are the leader, and when things go wrong, you are to take the blame for the entire team. Accept the faults on behalf of the group, and go back to the team to share the feedback and re-strategize on new approaches for solving the problem. Choosing to become a manager is getting ready to have your time consumed. Earlier in the book, I stated that management is mostly people management, and people management is never easy. You are a team leader with a team. All work has to pass through you and gain your approval before being submitted or used.

This process is never easy. Imagine working with a group of nine. You have to oversee nine workloads that include yours. That is ten in total. You are laden with ten workloads that all have deadlines. These deadlines must be met, work supervised, meetings fixed and attended, and so many impromptu activities that might arise. All these would take your time and would require your utmost concentration and skills. It is very time-consuming.

Do not also forget you have a personal life outside work, and they are both one life. Time management is a skill you need to learn to meet your goals at the assigned time desperately.

Be ready to experience a shift in focus. Before becoming a manager, you would have been overseeing several projects that only require an individual thought process. When you become a manager, it is different. You are required to see and access situations from different perspectives. This job is a new higher position that needs you to oversee, coordinate, and conduct a much bigger picture. You would have new problems to solve. You would be managing meetings, budgets, customer complaints, and many others. It is a new world that would need you to wear a new lens to view it.

When I first started as a manager, I told myself, "easy bitty. It shouldn't be that difficult. I was born for this." I was wrong in thinking it would be an easy phase and the first few months were the hardest on me. I fought so hard to stay afloat till I realized I wasn't tapping into the bigger picture. I was letting myself be myopic and not embrace the newfound changes. I thought I knew it all, and I was ready till I was finally in that position. I learned not only to shift my focus but tap into the bigger picture I blindly ignored. So yes! Be ready for that shift. Wear your armor and take the bull by its horns. When someone expresses an interest to become manager, I suggest the following:

Be ready to become accountable

Becoming a manager means being accountable for the work of your team. Many people end up underperforming as managers because they never really wanted to be a manager in the first place — as a consequence, they don't put in the time to learn how it's done. They never know how to be genuinely accountable.

Be ready to handle conflicts

There are people out there who don't run and hide when conflict comes to town. So, if you're planning on becoming a manager, it'll be best for everyone involved if you're part of the former group rather than the latter. You should be ready to handle various types of conflicts and resolve them with patience.

Be ready to care about people deeply

It is not motivating to work under a manager who does not care. Caring manager - Listen and address the problems; the caring manager provides actionable feedback where and when necessary. Caring managers are great listeners; they appreciate your effort and the outcome when you pull off something unique. You need to care deeply about your team members while not worrying much about what they think about you.

Be ready to love people

Managers, many of the time, spend a full day in back-to-back 1:1s talking to people. Does that sound awful or awesome? People management is not an added responsibility when you become a manager. It is one of the most critical responsibilities. You need to deliver the business results through your team. Being a manager means that there are times when you are dealing with people's problems more than with technical problems. Technical problems are challenging, but people's problems are even harder, long-winding, ever-recurring, and completely irrational. Be prepared to catch yourself thinking: "God, am I in kindergarten? I should not have to deal with this!"

	Myth	**Reality**
Describe Manager role	Authority "Now, I will have the freedom to make a decision."	Responsibility "I have the responsibility of my team and work my team has to deliver."
Source of power	Formal authority "I am most powerful in the team."	Earn trust "I need to earn the trust of my team."
Managerial focus	Managing one-to-one "My role is to build relationships with each of my team members."	Leading the team "I need to foster a culture that will allow the team to fulfill its potential."
Key challenges	Keeping the projects on track "My job is to make sure that projects get delivered on time."	Improve my team's performance "I am responsible for initiating changes to improve my team's performance."

However, if you refuse to tackle people's issues, then your team will fall apart. In these situations, it helps a lot if you love dealing with people.

CHAPTER SUMMARY

You are always making a choice; even a seeming lack of choice is a choice. Always make it count. As a manager, you must learn to be uncomfortable. As a leader, you must be ready to master the challenging skill of people management. As a manager, you must be ready to take on enormous responsibilities as they come. It is essential to have guiding principles that will help you on your way to achieving success. Choosing to become a manager is not easy, but it is worth it. Make the choice today!

REFLECTIONS

Why do you think you can be a good manager? List all the good quality of a good manager you have?
Reflect:
_____
_____
_____
_____

Are you already being viewed as a manager in the organization, and if offered the position, would you be ready to step up and officially take on that role?

Reflect:
_____
_____
_____
_____

As a manager, what are your guiding principles to help your team achieve success?
Reflect:
_____
_____
_____
_____

CHAPTER 9

JUST START

"Don't let perfectionism become an excuse for never getting started."

- Marilu Henner

A journey of a thousand miles indeed begins with a single step. All endeavors in life require actions to achieve. For a lot of people, the fear of starting hinders them from achieving their goals. The hardest part of accomplishing anything in life is starting; then, it becomes manageable. As previously discussed in the book, you must be proactive and have a growth mindset. You should also understand that you will learn to deal with challenges after starting the journey.

There is no such thing as the perfect plan. Life will continue to bring new challenges your way that will ultimately help your growth process. We all had that perfect picture where we had the perfect grades, graduated with the perfect score, got hired by our dream company, married the perfect partner, and had the ideal family.

These were lofty dreams, but we soon realized life had other plans for us. Most of us didn't get what we hoped for, but we learned to explore and adapt to other options. The journey of life is never straightforward.

The same logic applies to starting your journey as a manager in whatever capacity. You should understand that it will not be a smooth ride to paradise, but that should not deter you from starting anyway. If you have read the book to this chapter, now is the time to take action because reading without action is futile. The way inspiration without action is just a thought. This book's aim is ultimately defeated if you do not start bringing the right changes in your management style to help you get the best out of your team members and progress towards becoming a best manager. That idea you think will enhance your team's productivity or the idea that will make your team members more valuable.

You started the journey by understanding who a manager is, the best qualities of a manager, how to manage your team remotely, building the ideal culture of diversity, psychological safety, and teamwork in your group, how to connect the dots by having moments of strategic pause. Now, it is time to take steps to achieve your goals and thrive in your role.

"Have a bias for action - let's see something happen now. You can break that big plan into small steps and take the first step right away."
- **Indira Gandhi, Indian Statesman**

As a manager, you will have many duties and tasks to perform. These tasks all require your utmost attention. They also include deadlines that you must meet. Some of these tasks to be completed might have the same deadlines, and it is a prerequisite that they are all submitted whether or not you think there isn't enough time. A manager always remembers the importance of deadlines.

You will have lots of responsibilities that need to be excellently put together and submitted on the due dates. The words commitments and manager intertwine. They are inseparable elements that must blend in the right proportion.

JUST START

So, what do you do when you face these responsibilities? Do you break down, or do you fight hard enough to deliver outstandingly, or do you quake under pressure?

Do you let yourself start the project regardless, or are you the person to go round in circles doing everything yet nothing? Just start is the chapter for you that explains why you need to go ahead with that project and do what you have to do.

Sometime in 2015, I faced significant difficulties that had me up for many nights. I had to handle an enormous project that felt insurmountable. If successfully executed by my team members and me, the project would mean a bigger and better reputation and recognition for my company. It would also imply that we were capable and reliable as a team, which put me under immense pressure to deliver.

Handling the project wasn't an issue, as I have had several relevant experiences under my belt as a professional in my field. Starting the project was where the problem laid. I did not know how to start. I remember instructing my team members to do extensive research for the project. In less than a week, everyone's research was ready. Yet, we all did not know how to start this project. It was like a student writing a letter and not knowing which was to be the heading, body, or conclusion of the message.

Many days had passed, and we drew closer to our deadline. Few days before our closing date, I walked into the office and announced we were starting this project, and however it ended up, we were going to do our best. I refused to let the fear and anxiety of the project eat me up any longer.

We proceeded, and it surprisingly turned out much better than we expected it to be. It was glorious, and if you ask me, it turned out to be one of the best moments in my professional life. We did not only deliver, but we also added a new creative side to the project that made it exceedingly unique. The company rewarded our efforts with extra benefits and a raise in our earnings. What valuable message did I take from this project, you may ask yourself?

I took the lesson of "starting." And, this lesson has further shaped and molded my career into what it is today.

As a manager, you will face a myriad of deadlines and projects. That is a mandate. Some projects may not come easy and may leave me in a constant state of confusion on how to proceed on the project further, and my one singular advice is; start! You do not need all the information before you can begin; you learn more as you make progress. Fail fast, change the course, and keep going. Keep moving; as I said, progress is more important than the outcome. If you can move along with your team, then success is inevitable.

Do not overthink the situation; do not wonder about your performance or how the result might end up looking, do not do any of these. When you face a difficult situation, hold on to it, don't react, ponder on it, then act and respond to it.

What you need to do is to start working on the project. Many managers make the mistake of assuming that clarity is more significant than actions when starting a new project. It is why many spend so much time thinking than doing. And when you spend more time thinking than doing, be rest assured that you would only be mounting more pressure on yourself and your team members. "But is clarity not important as well?" of course, yes, it is important!

Clarity is crucial, but on a scale of preference when handling jobs that require your attention with a limited time frame, actions are more important, and more clarity comes after efforts. Clarity comes on the way while performing those actions. It is like reading a book. When you open up a book to read, you do not immediately grasp the book's message in one read; it takes several reads into many pages to get the message the author or writer is trying to pass across. Sometimes the message might not even be apparent until you finish reading that book. It is what actions and clarity mean.

Going to the bookshop, establishing time to read, and opening up a book to read are actions you have carried out. Reading the book and getting to discover new facts and ideas is clarity. Steps and transparency are imperative. They are two factors that go hand in hand, but one comes first before the other. However, it would be best if you blended both finely in equal proportion.

"It is useless to desire more time if you are already wasting the little you have."

-James Allen

There is little or no time left for you as a manager. You have to make sure to take the bull by the horns to achieve anything. Your team members rely on you. Your customers depend on you. The organization itself relies on you.

Therefore, the actions you take must be quick and decisive. You should also note that steps must be taken in the right way and direction while being necessary. Do not take actions you know would be detrimental to the team and organization. Activities are also not carried alone by yourself. It is a collective effort by the team. It has been proved and recognized to sail forward.

Be ready for everything. As a manager, you must prepare yourself for everything and anything that comes your way. There will most likely be cases where impromptu projects that have not been planned for or thought on will surface. These projects can be given to you in a day, or two and feedback may be expected in the shortest of times.

I once had a task given to my team members and me in a day, and we're to provide feedback the next day. There was no time to contemplate anything; we just needed to start the project. We had to halt other ongoing projects for this project due to the urgency and limited time frame. We got down to business, barely having time for lunch that day.

Fortunately, enough, we were able to deliver remarkably. It was also another learning moment for everyone. You need to train yourself and your team members to work under pressure collectively in a healthy working environment. It will help and improve everyone's cognitive abilities.

Working under pressure and just starting is the push your team needs to always be on their toes. You must be ready to face any new challenges or difficulties as they come. Be ready. It saves you from mistakes that could be disadvantageous to you and your team members.

Learning to collaborate is part of equipping yourself for effectiveness, problem-solving, innovation, and life-long learning in an ever-changing networked economy."- Don Tapscott.

Always be ready for the next project. Be rest assured that some projects run simultaneously. The likelihood of this is inevitable as you go along with your professional life as a manager. Not only would you be in a constant state of moving from meeting to meeting, but you might also juggle more than two or at projects at once, and you must always deliver the ideal results with your team members.

You have to learn how to start. Start regardless of the difficulties you may encounter in the course of the project. Go ahead and make that bold step and move. You can do this. Remember to have positive affirmations. You keep your mindset in the right place, as these play their part by acting as an encouragement tool to motivate you.

People are not born with a bias for action attitude. It can be developed and teased out through habituation and continuously working on becoming better at acting on those ideas that interest us. You have to start. There should be no consideration, fear, or hesitation. Just start! Keep doing this and see the results that would materialize itself over time. If you have high-level goals, that's great, but don't forget the importance of taking smaller actions daily on smaller things to build confidence in starting new things.

The next step is creating a pattern. It would be best to have a strategy that would serve as a guiding tool for succeeding in all projects to be handled. Throughout my career, this has helped in achieving set goals. My routine is something I never do away with, as it has helped keep me in check, and it has always produced positive and excellent results.

I would be sharing my pattern, but you should have it at the back of your mind that what works for you might not work for others. That is why it is called "your way." Because it serves and works for you.

When presented with a new project, I try first to understand the problem in front of me, which typically takes me a few minutes to decipher, and I explore all angles of the project. I make sure to weigh my options, what steps should I take first, and what actions should I take later. Why is this project important, and what does it achieve? By the way, I have learned that to start something, "why" is a significant word, and a few "why" questions will bring some clarity.

The next step and pattern I take are limiting the scope of the problem. No matter how big a project might look or seem, it is vital to determine the scope. Doing this will assist you in creating foundations to start you on the right foot. With this, you know you aren't stepping out of line, and you can fully grasp and wrap your hands around the problem. Along the way, you can make adjustments during the project when you possess full clarity about the scope of the task.

Envisaging the scope is very important as failure to do this would cause many unforeseen issues in the future. Team members may begin to step out of line and work grossly misinterpreted if the scope isn't well-defined.

"When it is obvious that the goals cannot be reached, don't adjust the goals, adjust the action steps."
– Confucius

The next step to start is making a plan. That is, deciding what comes next and what doesn't. Making a plan knows that it could fail, but you are ready to try and start again, nonetheless. Making a plan also includes exploring other options at your disposal in case one fails.

As a manager, you must have plans A, B, C, and even D if necessary. It would be best if you didn't lack alternative strategies towards achieving your goal.

The final piece of the puzzle is starting a project. As a manager, your ability to think through situations and act fast sets you apart from others. Always remember that you are a leader with a team that looks up to you. Building your foundation as a manager is equally essential. Foundations are a massive part of the construction. Without a proper foundation laying, the building is prone to fast destruction.

Now relate this to your life as a manager. You need to set the right foundation for yourself and the project. The right foundation sets the entire pace for the project. You need to adopt the necessary skills to ensure that you set the ideal foundation and move in the right direction.

What is the right foundation? It is setting the right ambiance, researching and gathering the proper materials needed, setting meeting dates, meeting the deadlines, and many more.

Just starting is taking and placing yourself in a position where you confidently allow yourself to proceed and act upon projects assigned to you. Just starting requires you to be ready, confident, and being able to accept failures and criticism. It is the ability to take projects thrown at you boldly. Just start!

Remember

"Don't let perfectionism become an excuse for never getting started."

- Marilu Henner

So, are you ready to take charge of your life and be the best version of yourself? If yes, START now!

CHAPTER SUMMARY

In every endeavor in life, STARTING is the most crucial part. You must always expect challenges and even welcome them on your path to progress. The journey to becoming the best manager and human being never ends. You must be persistent in your pursuit of success. Every experience has a lesson; find it. Setting the right foundation is vital to attaining success. When you change your mindset, you change your life.

REFLECTIONS

What is a passion of yours you're yet to act on?
Reflect:

Do you have a hard time getting started, particularly with things that you don't enjoy doing?
Reflect:

Do you believe in "The best way to get something done is to begin?" Yes or No, and why?
Reflect:

What is the difference between where you are now and your ideal self? What is your plan to be that ideal?
Reflect:

ABOUT THE AUTHOR

Sharad Bajaj is the Head of Engineering at Amazon (AWS) and a former Microsoft Group Engineering Manager. He is a strategic and visionary leader with over 20 years of experience as a technologist leading global engineering teams. He is recognized for innovation, hiring and developing talent, building large scale enterprises and consumer products and services. Furthermore, he is committed to helping new and seasoned managers to develop innovative ways to lead and manage their team while being the best version of themselves.

Connect with me on Instagram: @Iamthinkingandyou

Connect with me on LinkedIn: Sharad Bajaj

For feedback and reviews email me at: drivetothrivebook@gmail.com

ACKNOWLEDGEMENTS

Writing a book is harder than I thought and more rewarding than I could have ever imagined. None of this would have been possible without the support of my wife **Aarti**. She has been always supportive for everything I could do and wants to do in my life. She stood by me during every decision I made and all my struggles and successes.

Writing a book about the story of your own experience is an amazing journey to the past. I'm forever indebted to **Manan Verma** and **Paper2Publish** team for their editorial help, keen insight, and on-going support in bringing my experiences to life through this book. It is because of their efforts and encouragement that I have a legacy to pass on to my family where one didn't exist before. To **Shruti Chauhan (Instagram:@anarkali_ki_art)** for Book Cover, Graphics and promotional designs. To all of my colleagues, managers and people I worked with at Microsoft and Amazon for the experiences that inspired me and shaped my career.

To my close friends, **Varun, Adhir, Shashi Nagpure, Manish Ojha, Siddharth Singh, Kunal Garg, Maninderjit Singh, Abhishek Thakur, Hemant Gaur, Sandeep & Shivani Verma, Preti & Gurpreet Singh, Mahesh Kamat, Rakesh Garg, Sapna Garg, Sid Arora, Sumit Kaur,** and to my Seattle Lions friends **Rajesh Fandan, Ranjit Ubbi, Amit Oberoi, Mukesh Oberoi, Ashmeet Oberoi, Tarun Seth, Rajneesh Grover, Sameer Lalwani, Sameer Doultani, Nitin Kanojia, Abhinav Chopra, Kamal Kurswani, Rajan Gandhi, Sunil Lakhiyani, Deepak Makkar** for brainstorming the book ideas, always believing in me, and encouraging me to write **Drive To Thrive** book.

PAPER-2-PUBLISH
Making Author's Journey Easy

Writing a book is the best way to build a legacy that lasts until the end of time and the best way to spread your story. Becoming an author is a creative task but can take a very long time if done without proper guidance. We at **Paper2Publish** provide that guidance.

    We are the ones who hold your hands and take you from paper to publish by providing you a platform to share your story and build a legacy that stands the test of time.

    Whether it is writing, editing, proofreading the book or designing cover, guidance, marketing, copyrights, and free publishing. We help you with everything and make you independent. So, you can become a truly self-published author all by yourself.

    We are grateful and thankful to **Sharad Bajaj** for letting us make his author's journey easy and create a legacy that will last until the end of time.

Register for a free session at:
www.paper2publish.co.in/free

For full list of services visit:
www.paper2publish.co.in/services

Follow us on Instagram: @paper2publish

www.ingramcontent.com/pod-product-compliance
Lightning Source LLC
Chambersburg PA
CBHW060831220526
45466CB00003B/1060